SHADOW WORK

Books by Ivan Illich

As this edition is being printed for both the American and British markets, we list US and British publications separately:

USA
Celebration of Awareness (1971, Doubleday)
Deschooling Society (1971, Harper & Row)
Tools for Conviviality (1973, Harper & Row)
Energy and Equity (1974, Harper, Torchbooks)
Medical Nemesis (1976, Pantheon, Bantam)
Toward a History of Needs (1978, Pantheon, Bantam)
Disabling Professions (with others, 1978, Marion Boyars)

Great Britain
Celebration of Awareness (1971, Calder & Boyars, Penguin)
Deschooling Society (1971, Calder & Boyars, Penguin)
Tools for Conviviality (1973, Calder & Boyars, Fontana)
Energy & Equity (1974, Calder & Boyars)
Medical Nemesis (1975, Calder & Boyars)
Limits to Medicine: Medical Nemesis – The Appropriation of Health (1976, Marion Boyars, Penguin)
Disabling Professions (with others, 1977, Marion Boyars)
The Right to Useful Unemployment (1978, Marion Boyars)

All titles originally published by Calder & Boyars are now reprinted by Marion Boyars

About the Author

IVAN ILLICH was born in 1926. He studied theology, philosophy and history. He was assistant pastor in an Irish-Puerto Rican parish in New York and vice-rector of the Catholic University of Puerto Rico. From 1962–1967 he directed research seminars at CIDOC in Cuernavaca where he still lives. He is the author of many books and articles published world-wide. He is currently teaching Medieval History in Germany.

SHADOW WORK

by Ivan Illich

MARION BOYARS · BOSTON · LONDON

Published simultaneously in the
United States, Canada and Great Britain 1981
by Marion Boyars Inc.
99 Main Street, Salem, New Hampshire 03079
and Marion Boyars Publishers Ltd.
18 Brewer Street, London W1R 4AS

Australian and New Zealand distribution by Thomas C. Lothian
4-12 Tattersalls Lane, Melbourne, Victoria 3000

Library of Congress Cataloging in Publication Data

Illich, Ivan D.
  Shadow work

  (Open forum series)
  Includes bibliographical references.
  1. Economic development—Social aspects—
Addresses, essays, lectures. 2. Economic anthro-
pology—Addresses, essays, lectures. 3. Subsistence
economy—Addresses, essays, lectures. I. Title.
HD75.I44   306′.3   80-28089
ISBN 0-7145-2710-6
ISBN 0-7145-2711-4 (pbk.)

British Library Cataloguing in Publication Data

Illich, Ivan
  Shadow work.
  1. Economics
  I. Title
  330.1   HB171

Printed and bound in the USA
by The Maple-Vail Book Manufacturing Group

Contents

Acknowledgments

Portions and different versions of the essays in this book were published in *Teachers College Record*, Columbia University, Volume 81, Number 1, Fall 1979, *Co-Evolution Quarterly*, Sausalito, California, No. 26, Summer 1980 (under the title *Vernacular Values*) and *The Guardian*, London, October 4, 1980.

Introduction

I am grateful to Marion Boyars for publishing this collection of essays in an original soft cover edition with just enough hard bound copies to satisfy librarians. These are indeed essays, or drafts. Each reports some aspect of the progress I have made on a book I shall finish within the next three years. Each was originally addressed to a different audience in 1979 and 1980. I have decided to publish them together now in order to call attention to an urgent issue without, however, rushing to a premature conclusion of my major study on the history of scarcity.

The essays gathered here deal with the rise of the shadow economy. I have coined this term to speak about transactions which are not in the monetized sector and yet do not exist in pre-industrial societies. The acquisition of taught mother tongue is an example on which I elaborate in this book.

From Karl Polanyi I take the idea that modern history can be understood as the 'disembedding' of a market economy. However, I do not analyze this uniquely modern, disembedded economy from the perspective in which the concepts of formal economics can be meaningfully applied to it. Rather, I am interested in its shadowy underside. I want to describe those of its features which escape both the categories of formal economics, and those which anthropology finds applicable in the study of subsistence cultures. Looking at early nineteenth century history, I find that with the progress of monetization a non-monetized and complementary hemi-sphere comes into existence. And both these hemi-spheres are equally, however differently, foreign to what prevails in pre-industrial societies. Both degrade the utilization value of the environment; both destroy subsistence.

With the rise of this shadow economy I observe the appearance of a kind of toil which is not rewarded by wages, and yet contributes nothing to the household's independence from the market. In fact, this new kind of activity, for which the shadow work of the housewife in her new non-subsistent domestic sphere, one prime example is a necessary condition for the family wage earner to exist. Thus shadow work, which is as recent a phenomenon as modern wage labor, might be even more fundamental than the latter for the continued existence of a commodity-intensive society. Its distinction from the vernacular activities typical for subsistence-oriented popular cultures is the most difficult and the most rewarding part of my research.

My study is not motivated by mere curiosity. I am moved by concern over a trend which manifested itself during the seventies. During this time professional, economic and political interests converged on an intense expansion of the shadow economy. As ten years ago Ford, Fiat and Volkswagen financed the Club of Rome to prophecy limits to growth, so they now urge the need for self-help. I consider the indiscriminate propagation of self-help to be morally unacceptable.

What is here propagated as self-help is the opposite of autonomous or vernacular life. The self-help the new economists preach divides the subject of social policy (be it a person or entity) into two halves: one that stands in a professionally defined need, and the other who is professionally licenced to provide it. Under the policies that are thus labelled as self-help, the apartheid of production and consumption, characteristic of industrial economics, is projected into the subject itself. Each one is turned into a production unit for internal consumption, and the utility derived from this masturbation is then added to a newfangled GNP. Unless we clarify the distinction between this self-help and what I shall call *vernacular life*, the shadow economy will become the main growth sector during the current stagflation, the 'informal' sector will become the main colony which sustains a last flurry of growth. And, unless the apostles of new life styles, of decentralization and alternative technology and conscientization and liberation make this distinction explicit and practical, they will only add some color, sweetener and the taste of stagnant ideals to an irresistibly spreading shadow economy.

The distinction I make between shadow work and the vernacular domain is thus not of merely academic importance.

The distinction is crucial to understand the third stage into which the public discussion on the limits to growth is just now entering.

The first stage occurred more than ten years ago. Then, newsmakers within the universities and in the media suddenly focused public attention on the obvious danger that soon the biosphere might be rendered uninhabitable unless the prevailing trends of industrial production were changed. The alarms stressed the physical environment, and the ensuing discussions tended to be monopolized by concerns about fuels and poisons. It seemed important, then, to call attention to the need for analogous limits in the service sector. This I tried to do with *Deschooling Society*. There I argued that the service agencies of the Welfare State inevitably lead to destructive side effects which can be compared to the unwanted side effects which result from the overproduction of goods. Limits on care had to be envisaged as the necessary complement to limits on goods. Further, both kinds of limits were fundamentally independent from political choices or technological fixes. In the meantime, such limits to care have been recognized: limits to the medicalization of health, to the institutionalization of learning, to the insurance of risks, to the intensity of media exposure, to the tolerance for professional social work and care – all now form part of the discussion on the 'ecology'.

With the Eighties, the discussion on the limits to growth is moving into a third stage. The first stage had focused primarily on goods, the second on care. The third is focussing on the commons.

Speaking of the commons, one immediately imagines meadows and woods. One thinks of the enclosure of pastures by which the lord excluded the peasant's single sheep, thereby depriving him of a means of existence marginal to the market, and forcing him into proto-industrial wage labor. One thinks of the destruction of what E. P. Thompson called the moral economy. The commons now under discussion are something much more subtle. Economists tend to speak about them as the 'utilization value of the environment'. I believe that in its third stage the public discussion on limits to economic growth will focus primarily on the preservation of these 'utilization values', values which are destroyed by economic expansion, *whatever* form it takes.

In principle, the reason for this is not difficult to understand. Up to now economic development has always meant that people, instead of doing something, are instead enabled to buy it. Use values beyond the market are replaced by commodities. Economic development has also meant that after a time people *must* buy the commodity, because the conditions under which they could get along without it had disappeared from their physical, social or cultural environment. And the environment could no longer be utilized by those who were unable to buy the good or service. Streets, for example, once were mainly for people. People grew up on them, and most became competent for life by what they learned there. Then streets were straightened and reshaped to serve vehicular traffic. And this change occurred long before schools were abundant enough to accommodate the young who were now driven from the streets. The utilization value of a formerly 'common' environment for learning disappeared much faster than it could be replaced by institutions for formal instruction.

In *Tools for Conviviality*, I called attention to how the environment is ruined for use-value oriented action by economic growth. I called this process the 'modernization of poverty' because in a modern society precisely those who have least access to the market also have least access to the utilization value of the commons. I ascribed this to the "radical monopoly of commodities over the satisfaction of needs".

Subsequently I tried to illustrate how this radical monopoly of commodities tends to remove entire populations from precisely those goals for which the production and general distribution of the product had been originally advocated. I chose the motorization of locomotion and the medicalization of health as my two prime examples for this paradoxical *counterproductivity*. In my next book I will trace the institutionalization of scarcity, Europe's most important contribution to the modern world, back to its origins in medieval beliefs.

In publishing these essays I am reporting on the progress of my study – but also reaching out for criticism and guidance. Each of these essays has its history: *The Dimensions of Public Choice* was first written at the request of Paul Streeten for delivery at the Conference of Development Economists in Colombo, Sri Lanka, in August 1979. The paper *The War*

Against Subsistence grew out of conversations with Devi P. Pattanayak, Director of the All India Institute of Languages in Mysore. *Research by People* is based on one of twelve lectures on texts of the early twelfth century given at the University of Kassel. I wrote it as my contribution to a reader on convivial tools which Valentina Borremans is preparing. It will appear there, along with contributions by Karl Polanyi, Lewis Mumford, André Gorz and others. The essay *Shadow Work* grew out of conversations with Barbara Duden and Claudia von Werlhof, as well as with Christine and Ernst von Weizsäcker. It was widely used as an outline for seminars both within and outside universities in late 1980, and I now publish it with the draft of a study guide which I prepared for these students.

The entire text is the outcome of a conversation with Lee Hoinacki that now enters its third decade. He has edited the manuscript. I often cannot recall who coined which phrase, before or after it was first written down.

Ivan Illich
Göttingen, November 1980

I
THE THREE DIMENSIONS
OF PUBLIC CHOICE

WHERE the war against subsistence has led can best be seen in the mirror of so-called development. During the 1960's, 'development' acquired a status that ranked with 'freedom' and 'equality'. Other peoples' development became the rich man's duty and burden. Development was described as a building program – people of all colors spoke of 'nation-building' and did so without blushing. The immediate goal of this social engineering was the installation of a balanced set of equipment in a society not yet so instrumented: the building of more schools, more modern hospitals, more extensive highways, new factories, power grids, together with the creation of a population trained to staff and need them.

Today, the moral imperative of ten years ago appears naive; today, few critical thinkers would take such an instrumentalist view of the desirable society. Two reasons have changed many minds: first, undesired externalities exceed benefits – the tax burden of schools and hospitals is more than any economy can support; the ghost towns produced by highways impoverish the urban and rural landscape. Plastic buckets from Saõ Paulo are lighter and cheaper than those made of scrap by the local tinsmith in Western Brazil. But first cheap plastic puts the tinsmith out of existence, and then the fumes of plastic leave a special trace on the environment – a new kind of ghost. The destruction of age-old competence as well as these poisons are inevitable byproducts and will resist all exorcisms for a long time. Cemeteries for industrial waste simple cost too much, more than the buckets are worth. In economic jargon, the 'external costs' exceed not only the profit made from plastic bucket production, but also the very salaries paid in the manufacturing process.

These *rising externalities*, however, are only one side of the bill which development has exacted. *Counterproductivity is its reverse side*. Externalities represent costs that are 'outside' the price paid by the consumer for what he wants – costs that he, others or future generations will at some point be charged. Counterproductivity, however, is a new kind of disappointment which arises 'within' the very use of the good purchased. This internal counterproductivity, an inevitable component of modern institutions, has become the constant frustration of the poorer majority of each institution's clients: intensely experienced but rarely defined. Each major sector of the economy produces its own unique and paradoxical contradictions. Each necessarily brings about the opposite of that for which it was structured. Economists, who are increasingly competent to put price-tags on externalities, are unable to deal with negative internalities, and cannot measure the inherent frustration of captive clients, which is something other than a cost. For most people, schooling twists genetic differences into certified degradation; the medicalization of health increases demand for services far beyond the possible and useful, and undermines that organic coping ability which common sense calls health; transportation, for the great majority bound to the rush hour, increases the time spent in the servitude to traffic, reducing both freely chosen mobility and mutual access. The development of educational, medical and other welfare agencies has actually removed most clients from the obvious purpose for which these projects were designed and financed. This institutionalized frustration, resulting from compulsory consumption, combined with the new externalities, totally discredit the description of the desirable society in terms of installed production capacity. As a result, slowly, the full impact of industralization on the environment becomes visible: while only some forms of growth threaten the biosphere, all economic growth threatens the 'commons'. All economic growth inevitably degrades the utilization value of the environment.

Defense against the damages inflicted by development, rather than giving access to some new 'satisfaction', has become the most sought after privilege. You have arrived if you can commute outside the rush hour; have probably attended an elite school if you can give birth at home; are privy to rare and special knowledge if you can bypass the physician when you are ill; are rich and lucky if you can breathe fresh air; not really poor if you can build your own shack. The underclasses are now made up of those who *must* consume the counterproductive packages and ministrations of their self-appointed tutors; the privileged are those who are free to refuse them. A new attitude, then, has taken shape during these last years: the awareness that we cannot ecologically afford *equitable* development leads many to understand that, even if development in equity were possible, we would neither want more of it for ourselves, nor want to suggest it for others.

Ten years ago, we tended to distinguish social options exercised within the political sphere from technical options assigned to the expert. The former were meant to focus on goals, the latter more on means. Roughly, options about the desirable society were ranged on a spectrum that ran from right to left: here, capitalist, over there, social 'development'. The *how* was left to the experts. This one-dimensional model of politics is now passé. Today, in addition to 'who gets what', two new areas of choice have become *lay* issues: the very legitimacy of lay judgment on the apt means for production, and the trade-offs between growth and freedom. As a result, three independent classes of options appear as three mutually perpendicular axes of public choice. On the x-axis I place the issues related to social hierarchy, political authority, ownership of the means of production and allocation of resources that are usually designated by the terms 'right' and 'left'. On the y-axis, I place the technical choices between 'hard' and 'soft', extending these terms far beyond a pro and con atomic power: not only goods, but also services are affected by the hard and soft alternatives.

A third choice falls on the z-axis. Neither privilege nor technique, but rather the nature of human satisfaction is at issue. To characterize the two extremes, I shall use terms defined by Erich Fromm. At the bottom, I place a social organization that fits the seeking of satisfaction in *having*; at the top, in *doing*. At the bottom, therefore, I place a commodity-intensive society where needs are increasingly defined in terms of packaged goods and services designed and prescribed by professionals, and produced under their control. This social ideal corresponds to the image of a humanity composed of individuals, each driven by considerations of marginal utility, the image that has developed from Mandeville via Smith and Marx to Keynes, and

that Louis Dumont calls *homo economicus*. At the opposite end, at
the top of the z-axis, I place – in a fan-shaped array – a great
variety of societies where existence is organized around subsistence activities, each community choosing its unique life style
tempered by skepticism about the claims of growth. On this
z-axis of choice I do not oppose growth-oriented societies to
others in which traditional subsistence is structured by im-
memorial cultural transmission of patterns. Such a choice does
not exist. Aspirations of this kind would be sentimental and
destructive. I oppose to the societies in the service of economic
growth which I place at the bottom of the z-axis those which put
high value on the replacement of both production and consumption by the subsistence-oriented utilization of common
environments. I thus oppose societies organized in view of *homo
economicus* societies which have recovered the traditional assumptions about *homo artifix, subsistens*.

The shape of a contemporary society is in fact the result of
ongoing choices along these three independent axes. But due to
the current one-dimensional conception of politics, most of
these choices are the result of a synergy of unrelated decisions,
which all tend to organize the environment as a cage for *homo
economicus*. This trend is experienced by ever more people with
deep anxiety. Thus a polity's credibility begins to depend on the
degree of public participation in each of the three option sets.
The beauty of a unique, socially articulated image of each
society will, hopefully, become the determining factor of its
international impact. Esthetic and ethical example may replace
the competition of economic indicators. Actually, no other
route is open. A mode of life characterized by austerity, modesty,
modern yet hand-made and built on a small scale does not lend
itself to propagation through marketing. For the first time in
history, poor and rich societies would be effectively placed on
equal terms. But for this to become true, the present perception
of international north-south relations in terms of development
must first be superseded.

A related high status goal of our age, full employment, must
also be reviewed. Ten years ago, attitudes toward development
and politics were simpler than what is possible today; attitudes
toward work were sexist and naive. Work was identified with
employment, and prestigious employment confined to males.

The analysis of shadow work done off the job was taboo. The left referred to it as a remnant of primitive reproduction, the right, as organized consumption – all agreed that, with development, such labor would wither away. The struggle for more jobs, for equal pay for equal jobs, and more pay for every job pushed all work done off the job into a shadowed corner hidden from politics and economics. Recently, feminists, together with some economists and sociologists, looking at so-called intermediary structures, have begun to examine the unpaid contribution made to an industrial economy, a contribution for which women are principally responsible. These persons discuss 'reproduction' as the complement to production. But the stage is mostly filled with self-styled radicals who discuss new ways of creating conventional jobs, new forms of sharing available jobs and how to transform housework, education, childbearing and commuting into paid jobs. Under the pressure of such demands, the full employment goal appears as dubious as development. New actors, who question the very nature of work, advance toward the limelight. They distinguish industrially structured work, paid or unpaid, from the creation of a livelihood beyond the confines of employment and professional tutors. Their discussions raise the key issues on the vertical axis. The choice for or against the notion of man as a growth addict decides whether unemployment, that is, the effective liberty to work free from wages and/or salary, shall be viewed as sad and a curse, or as useful and a right.

In a commodity-intensive society, basic needs are met through the products of wage labor – housing no less than education, traffic no less than the delivery of infants. The work ethic which drives such a society legitimates employment for salary or wages and degrades independent coping. But the spread of wage labor accomplishes more – it divides unpaid work into two opposite types of activities. While the loss of unpaid work through the encroachment of wage labor has often been described, the creation of a new kind of work has been consistently ignored: the unpaid *complement* of industrial labor and services. A kind of forced labor or industrial serfdom in the service of commodity-intensive economies must be carefully distinguished from subsistence-oriented work lying outside the industrial system. Unless this distinction is clarified and used when choosing options on the z-axis, unpaid work guided by professionals could spread through a repressive, ecological welfare society. Women's serfdom in the domestic sphere is the most obvious example today. Housework is not salaried. Nor is it a subsistence activity in the sense that most of the work done by women was such as when, with their menfolk, they used the entire household as the setting and the means for the creation of most of the inhabitants' livelihood. Modern housework is standardized by industrial commodities oriented toward the support of production, and exacted from women in a sex-specific way to press them into reproduction, regeneration and a motivating force for the wage laborer. Well publicized by feminists, housework is only one expression of that extensive shadow economy which has developed everywhere in industrial societies as a necessary complement to expanding wage labor. This shadow complement, together with the formal economy, is a constitutive element of the industrial mode of production. It has escaped economic analysis, as did the wave nature of elementary particles before the Quantum Theory. And when concepts developed for the formal economic sector are applied to it, they distort what they do not simply miss. The real difference between two kinds of unpaid activity – shadow work which complements wage labor, and subsistence work which competes with and opposes both – is consistently missed. Then, as subsistence activities become more rare, all unpaid activities assume a structure analogous to housework. Growth-oriented work inevitably leads to the standardization and management of activities, be they paid or unpaid.

A contrary view of work prevails when a community chooses a subsistence-oriented way of life. There, the inversion of development, the replacement of consumer goods by personal action, of industrial tools by convivial tools is the goal. There, both wage labor and shadow work will decline since their product, goods or services, is valued primarily as a means for ever inventive activities, rather than as an end, that is, dutiful consumption. There, the guitar is valued over the record, the library over the schoolroom, the backyard garden over the supermarket selection. There, the personal control of each worker over his means of production determines the small horizon of each enterprise, a horizon which is a necessary condition for social production and the unfolding of each worker's individuality. This mode of production also exists in slavery, serfdom and other forms of dependence. But it flourishes, releases its energy, acquires its adequate and classical form *only* where the worker is the free owner of his tools and resources; only then can the artisan perform like a virtuoso. This mode of production can be maintained only within the limits that nature dictates to both production and society. There, useful unemployment is valued while wage labor, within limits, is merely tolerated.

The development paradigm is more easily repudiated by those who were adults on January 10, 1949. That day, most of us met the term in its present meaning for the first time when President Truman announced his Point Four Program. Until then, we used 'development' to refer to species, real estate and moves in chess – only thereafter to people, countries and economic strategies. Since then, we have been flooded by development theories whose concepts are now curiosities for collectors – 'growth', 'catching up', 'modernization', 'imperialism', 'dualism', 'dependency', 'basic needs', 'transfer of technology', 'world system', 'autochthonous industrialization' and 'temporary unlinking'. Each onrush came in two waves. One carried the pragmatist who highlighted free enterprise and world markets; the other, the politicians who stressed ideology and revolution. Theorists produced mountains of prescriptions and mutual caricatures. Beneath these, the common assumptions of all were buried. Now is the time to dig out the axioms hidden in the idea of development itself.

Fundamentally, the concept implies the replacement of widespread, unquestioned competence at subsistence activites by the use and consumption of commodities; the monopoly of wage labor over all other kinds of work; redefinition of needs in terms of goods and services mass-produced according to expert design; finally, the rearrangement of the environment in such fashion that space, time, materials and design favor production and consumption while they degrade or paralyze use-value oriented activities that satisfy needs directly. And all such worldwide homogeneous changes and processes are valued as inevitable and good. The great Mexican muralists dramatically portrayed the typical figures before the theorists outlined the stages. On their walls, one sees the ideal type of human being as the male in overalls behind a machine or in a white coat over a microscope. He tunnels mountains, guides tractors, fuels smoking chimneys. Women give him birth, nurse and teach him. In striking contrast to Aztec subsistence, Rivera and Orozco visualize industrial work as the sole source of all the goods needed for life and its possible pleasures.

But this ideal of industrial man now dims. The taboos that protected it weaken. Slogans about the dignity and joy of wage labor sound tinny. Unemployment, a term first introduced in 1898 to designate people without a fixed income, is now recognized as the condition in which most of the world's people live anyway – even at the height of industrial booms. In Eastern Europe especially, but also in China, people now see that, since 1950, the term 'working class' has been used mainly as a cover to claim and obtain privileges for a new bourgeoisie and its children. The 'need' to create employment and stimulate growth, by which the self-appointed paladins of the poorest have so far squashed any consideration of alternatives to development, clearly appears suspect.

The challenges to development take multiple forms. In Germany alone, France or Italy, thousands of groups experiment, each differently, with alternatives to an industrial existence. Increasingly, more of these people come from blue-collar homes. For most of them, there is no dignity left in earning one's livelihood by a wage. They try to "unplug themselves from consumption", in the phrase of some South Chicago slum-dwellers. In the USA, at least four million people live in the core of tiny and highly differentiated communities of this kind, with at least seven times as many individually sharing their values – women seek alternatives to gynecology; parents alternatives to schools; home-builders alternatives to the flush toilet; neighborhoods alternatives to commuting; people alternatives to the shopping center. In Trivandrum, South India, I have seen one of the most successful alternatives to a special kind of commodity dependence – to instruction and certification as the privileged forms of learning. One thousand seven hundred villages have installed libraries, each containing at least a thousand titles. This is the minimum equipment they need to be full members of Kerala Shastra Sahitya Parishad, and they may retain their membership only as long as they loan at least three thousand volumes per year. I was immensely encouraged to see that, at least in South India, village-based and village-financed libraries have turned schools into adjuncts to libraries, while elsewhere libraries during these last ten years have become mere deposits for teaching materials used under the instruction of professional teachers. Also in Bihar, India, Medico International represents a grassroots-based attempt to de-medicalize health care, without falling into the trap of the Chinese barefooted doctor. The latter has been relegated to the lowest level lackey in a national hierarchy of bio-control.

Besides taking such experiential forms, the challenge to development also uses legal and political means. In an Austrian referendum an absolute majority refused permission to Chancellor Kreisky, politically in control of the electorate, to inaugurate a finished atomic generator. Citizens increasingly use the ballot and the courts, in addition to more traditional interest group pressures, to set negative design criteria for the technology of production. In Europe, 'green' candidates now influence elections. In America, citizen legal efforts begin to stop highways and dams. Such behavior was not predictable ten years ago – and many men in power still do not recognize it as legitimate. All these grassroots-organized lives and actions in the Metropolis challenge not only the recent concept of overseas development, but also the more fundamental and root concept of progress and of 'needs' at home.

At this juncture, it is the task of the historian and the philosopher to clarify the sources of and disentangle the process resulting in Western needs. Only thus shall we be able to understand how such a seemingly enlightened concept produced such devastating exploitation. Progress, the notion which has characterized the West for 2000 years, and has determined its relations to outsiders since the decay of classical Rome, lies behind the belief in needs. Societies mirror themselves not only in their transcendent gods, but also in their image of the alien beyond their frontiers. The West exported a dichotomy between 'us' and 'them' unique to industrial society. This peculiar attitude toward self and others is now worldwide, constituting the victory of a universalist mission initiated in Europe. A redefinition of development would only reinforce the Western economic domination over the shape of formal economics by the professional colonization of the informal sector, domestic and foreign. To eschew this danger, the six-stage metamorphosis of a concept that currently appears as 'development' must first be understood.

Every community has a characteristic attitude toward others. The Chinese, for example, cannot refer to the alien or his chattel without labeling them with a degrading marker. For the Greek, he is either the house guest from a neighboring polis, or the barbarian who is less than fully man. In Rome, barbarians could become members of the city, but to bring them into it was never the intent or mission of Rome. Only during late antiquity, with the Western European Church, did the alien become someone in need, someone to be brought in. This view of the alien as a burden has become constitutive for Western society; without this universal mission to the world outside, what we call the West would not have come to be.

The perception of the outsider as someone who must be helped has taken on successive forms. In late antiquity, the barbarian mutated into the pagan – the second stage toward development had begun. The pagan was defined as the unbaptized, but ordained by nature to become Christian. It was the duty of those within the Church to incorporate him by baptism into the body of Christendom. In the early Middle Ages, most people in Europe were baptized, even though they might not yet be converted. Then the Muslim appeared. Unlike Goths and Saxons, Muslims were monotheists, and obviously prayerful believers; they resisted conversion. Therefore, besides baptism, the further needs to be subjected and instructed had to be imputed. The pagan mutated into the infidel, our third stage. By the late Middle Ages, the image of the alien mutated again. The Moors had been driven from Granada, Columbus had sailed across the ocean, and the Spanish Crown had assumed many functions of the Church. The image of the wild man who threatens the civilizing function of the humanist replaced the image of the infidel who threatens the faith. At this time also, the alien was first described in economy-related terms. From many studies on monsters, apes and wild men, we learn that the Europeans of this period saw the wild man as having no needs. This independence made him noble, but a threat to the designs of colonialism and mercantilism. To impute needs to the wild man, one had to make him over into the native, the fifth stage. Spanish courts, after long deliberation, decided that at least the native of the New World had a soul and was, therefore, human. In opposition to the wild man, the native has needs, but needs unlike those of civilized man. His needs are fixed by climate, race, religion and providence. Adam Smith still reflects on the elasticity of native needs. As Gunnar Myrdal has observed, the construct of distinctly native needs was necessary both to justify colonialism and to administer colonies. The provision of government, education and commerce for the natives was for four hundred years the white man's assumed burden.

Each time the West put a new mask on the alien, the old one was discarded because it was now recognized as a caricature of an abandoned self-image. The pagan with his naturally Christian soul had to give way to the stubborn infidel to allow Christendom to launch the Crusades. The wild man became necessary to justify the need for secular humanist education. The native was the crucial concept to promote self-righteous colonial rule. But by the time of the Marshall Plan (after World War II), when multinational conglomerates were expanding and the ambitions of transnational pedagogues, therapists and planners knew no bounds, the natives' limited needs for goods and services thwarted growth and progress. They had to metamorphose into underdeveloped people, the sixth and present stage of the West's view of the outsider. Thus decolonization was also a process of conversion: the worldwide acceptance of the Western self-image of *homo economicus* in his most extreme form as *homo industrialis*, with all needs commodity-defined. Scarcely twenty years were enough to make two billion people define themselves as underdeveloped. I vividly remember the Rio Carnival of 1963 – the last before the Junta imposed itself. 'Development' was the motif in the prize-winning samba, 'development' the shout of the dancers while they jumped to the throbbing of the drums.

Development based on high per capita energy quanta and intense professional care is the most pernicious of the West's missionary efforts – a project guided by an ecologically unfeasible conception of human control over nature, and by an anthropologically vicious attempt to replace the nests and snakepits of culture by sterile wards for professional service. The hospitals that spew out the newborn and reabsorb the dying, the schools run to busy the unemployed before, between and after jobs, the apartment towers where people are stored between trips to the supermarkets, the highways connecting garages form a pattern tatooed into the landscape during the short development spree. These institutions, designed for lifelong bottle babies wheeled from medical center to school to office to stadium begin now to look as anomalous as cathedrals, albeit unredeemed by any esthetic charm.

Ecological and anthropological realism are now necessary – but with caution. The popular call for soft is ambiguous; both right and left appropriate it. On the z-axis, it equally serves a honied beehive, or the pluralism of independent actions. The soft choice easily permits a recasting of a maternal society at home and another metamorphosis of missionary zeal abroad. For example, Amory Lovins argues that the possibility of further growth now depends on a rapid transition to the soft path. Only in this way, he claims, can the real income of rich countries double and that of poor countries triple in this generation. Only by the transition from fossil to sun can the externalities of production be so cut that the resources now spent on making waste and hiring scavengers to remove it be turned into benefits. I agree. If growth is to be, then Lovins is right; and investments are more secure with windspinners than with oil derricks. For the traditional right *and* left, for managerial democrats *or* socialist authoritarians, soft process and energy become the necessary rationale to expand their bureaucracies and to satisfy escalating 'needs' through the standardized production of goods and services.

The World Bank makes the matching argument for services. Only by choosing labor-intensive, sometimes less efficient forms of industrial production can education be incorporated in apprenticeship. More efficient plants create huge and costly externalities in the formal education they presuppose, while they cannot teach on the job.

The World Health Organization now stresses prevention and

education for self-care. Only thus can population health levels be raised, while expensive therapies – mostly of unproven effectiveness, although still the principal work of physicians – can be abandoned. The liberal egalitarian utopia of the eighteenth century, taken up as the ideal for industrial society by the socialists of the 19th, now seems realizable only on the soft and self-help path. On this point, right and left converge. Wolfgang Harich, a highly cultured communist, refined and steeled in his convictions by two stretches of eight years in solitary confinement – once under Hitler and once under Ulbricht – is the one East European spokesman for the soft path. But while for Lovins the transition to decentralized production depends on the market for Harich the necessity of this transition is an argument in favor of Stalinist ecology. For right *and* left, democrats *or* authoritarians, soft process and energy become the necessary means to satisfy escalating 'needs' through the standardized production of goods and services.

Thus, the soft path can lead either toward a convivial society where people are so equipped to do on their own whatever they judge necessary for survival and pleasure, or toward a new kind of commodity-dependent society where the goal of full employment means the political management of activities, paid or unpaid. Whether a 'left' or 'soft' path leads toward or away from new forms of 'development' and 'full employment' depends on the options taken between 'having' and 'being' on the third axis.

We have seen that wherever wage labor expands, its shadow, industrial serfdom, also grows. Wage labor, as the dominant form of production, and housework, as the ideal type of its unpaid complement, are both forms of activity without precedent in history or anthropology. They thrive only where the absolute and, later, the industrial state destroyed the social conditions for subsistence living. They spread as small-scale, diversified, vernacular communities have been made sociologically and legally impossible – into a world where individuals, throughout their lives, live only through dependence on education, health services, transportation and other packages provided through the multiple mechanical feeders of industrial institutions.

Conventional economic analysis has focused on only one of these complementary industrial age activities. Economic analysis has focused on the worker as wage earning producer. The

equally commodity-oriented activities performed by the unemployed have remained in the shadow of the economic searchlight. What women or children do, what occupies men after
'working hours', is belittled in a cavalier fashion. But this is
changing rapidly. Both the weight and the nature of the contribution made by unpaid activities to the industrial system begin
to be noticed. Feminist research into the history and anthropology of work has made it impossible to ignore the fact that
work in an industrial society is sex-specific in a manner which
cuts deeper than in any other known society. In the nineteenth
century, women entered the wage labor force in the 'advanced'
nations; they then won the franchise, non-restricted access to
schooling, equal rights on the job. All these 'victories' have had
precisely the opposite effect from that which conventional wisdom assigns them. Paradoxically, 'emancipation' has heightened
the contrast between paid and unpaid work; it has severed all
connections between unpaid work and subsistence. Thus, it has
redefined the structure of unpaid work so that this latter becomes
a new kind of serfdom inevitably borne by women.

Gender-specific tasks are not new; all known societies assign
sex-specific work roles. For example, hay may be cut by men,
raked by women, gathered by men, loaded by women, carted
away by men, fed to cows by women and to horses by men. But
no matter how much we search other cultures, we cannot find
the contemporary division between two forms of work, one paid
and the other unpaid, one credited as productive and the other
concerned with reproduction and consumption, one considered
heavy and the other light, one demanding special qualifications
and the other not, one given high social prestige and the other
relegated to 'private' matters. Both are equally fundamental
in the industrial mode of production. They differ in that the
surplus from paid work is taxed directly by the employer, while
the added value of unpaid work reaches him only via wage
work. Nowhere can we find this economic division of the sexes
through which surplus is created and expropriated.

This division between unpaid work off the job and paid work
through employment would have been unthinkable in societies
where the whole house served as a framework in which its
inhabitants, to a large extent, did and made those things by
which they also lived. Although we can find traces of both wage

work and its shadow in many societies, in none could either become the society's paradigm of work, nor be used as the key symbol for sex-specific tasks. And since two such types of work did not exist, the family did not have to exist to couple these kinds of opposites. Nowhere in history is the family, nuclear or extended, the instrument for linking two complementary but mutually exclusive species of work, one assigned primarily to the male, the other to the female. This symbiosis between opposite forms of activity, inseparably wedded through the family, is unique to commodity-intensive society. We now see that it is the inevitable result of the pursuit of development and full employment. And since such kinds of work did not exist, sex roles could not be defined with such finality, distinct natures could not be attributed to male and female, families could not be transformed into a solder to weld the two together.

An unsentimental history of industrial work thus removes the blindspot of economics: *homo economicus* has never been sexually neutral; from the beginning *he* was created as a couple, as *vir laborans*, the workingman, and *femina domestica*, the hausfrau, *homo industrialis* was made. In no society that developed toward the goal of full employment has shadow work not grown apace with that employment. And shadow work provided a device, effective beyond every precedent, to degrade a type of activity in which women cannot but predominate, while it supported one which privileged men.

Quite recently, the orthodox distinction between production and consumption functions ceased to hold. Suddenly, opposing interests turn the importance of unpaid work into a public issue. Economists put shadow prices on what happens in the 'informal' sector: the contribution that the work done by the client in choosing, paying for and carrying his cake adds to the value of the cake; the calculus of marginal choices made in sexual activities; the value of jogging over heart surgery. Housewives now claim pay for housework at the rate for such services in motels and restaurants. Teachers transmogrify mothers into trained but unpaid supervisors of their own children's homework. Government reports recognize that basic needs as professionally defined can be met only if laymen also produce these services, with competence but without pay. If growth and full employment retain their status as goals, the management of disciplined people motivated by non-monetary rewards will open up as the latest form of 'development' in the 1980's. *Homo industrialis*, now in blue jeans, aspires to economic unisex.

Rather than life in a shadow economy, I propose, on top of the z-axis, the ideas of 'vernacular work' unpaid activities which provide and improve livelihood, but which are totally refractory to any analysis utilizing concepts developed in formal economics. I apply the term '*vernacular*' to these activities, since there is no other current concept that allows me to make the same distinction within the domain covered by such terms as 'informal sector', 'use-value', 'social reproduction'. Vernacular is a Latin term that we use in English only for the language that we have acquired without paid teachers. In Rome, it was used from 500 B.C. to 600 A.D. to designate any value that was homebred, homemade, derived from the commons, and that a person could protect and defend though he neither bought nor sold it on the market. I suggest that we restore this simple term 'vernacular' to oppose commodities and their shadow. It allows me to distinguish between the expansion of the shadow economy and its inverse – the expansion of the vernacular domain.

The tension and balance between vernacular work and industrial labor – paid and unpaid – is the key issue on the third dimension of options, distinct from political right and left and from technical soft and hard. Industrial labor, paid and otherwise exacted, will not disappear. But when development, wage labor and its shadow encroach upon vernacular work the relative priority of one or the other constitutes the issue. We are free to choose between hierarchically managed standardized work that may be paid or unpaid, self-selected or imposed on the one hand and, on the other, we can protect our freedom to choose ever newly invented forms of simple, integrated subsistence actions which have an outcome that is unpredictable to the bureaucrat, unmanageable by hierarchies and oriented to the values shared within a specific community.

If the economy expands, which the soft choice might permit, the shadow economy cannot but grow even faster, and the vernacular domain must further decline. In this case, with rising job scarcity, the unemployed will be integrated into newly organized useful activities in the informal sector. Unemployed men will be given the so-called privilege to engage in those production-fostering types of unpaid activity that, since their emergence as housework in the nineteenth century, have been considerately earmarked for the 'weaker sex' – a designation that was also first used at that time, when industrial serfdom rather than subsistence was defined as the task of women. 'Care' exacted for the sake of love will lose its sex-specific character, and in the process become manageable by the state.

Under *this* option, international development is here to stay. Technical aid to develop the informal sector overseas will reflect the new sexless unpaid domestication of the unemployed at home. The new experts pushing French rather than German self-help methods or windmill designs already crowd airports and conferences. The last hope of development bureaucracies lies in the development of shadow economies.

Many of the dissidents that I have mentioned take a stand against all this – against the use of soft technology that by its nature reduces the vernacular domain and increases professional controls over informal sector activities. These new vanguards conceive technical progress as one possible instrument to support a new type of value, neither traditional nor industrial, but both subsistence-oriented and rationally chosen. Their lives, with more and less success, express a critical sense of beauty, a particular experience of pleasure, a unique view of life cherished by one group, understood but not necessarily shared by the next. They have found that modern tools make it possible to subsist on activities which permit a variety of evolving life styles, and relieve much of the drudgery of old-time subsistence. They struggle for the freedom to expand the vernacular domain of their lives.

Examples from Travancore to Wales may soon free those majorities who were recently captivated by the modern 'demonstration model' of stupefying, sickening and paralyzing enrichment. But two conditions must be met. First, the mode of life resulting from a new relation between people and tools must be informed by the perception of man as *homo artifex* and not *homo industrialis*. Second, commodity-independent life styles must be shaped anew by each small community, and not be imposed. Communities living by predominantly vernacular values have nothing much to offer to others besides the attractiveness of their example. But the example of a poor society that enhances modern subsistence by vernacular work should be rather attractive to jobless males in a rich society now condemned, like their women, to social reproduction in an expanding shadow economy. The ability, however, not only to live in new ways, but to insist on this freedom demands that we clearly recognize what distinguishes the perception of *homo economicus* from all other human beings. To this end I choose the study of history as a privileged road.

II
VERNACULAR
VALUES

It is human to see the environment made up of three kinds of things: foods, proscribed edibles and non-food. For a Hindu pork is taboo; not so begonias. These he has never thought of eating. By eating pork he loses caste. If however, he joins an Indio from central Mexico eating begonia flowers not he, but the world around him, has changed. Begonias have moved from non-food to food.

Issues as well can be thus divided. Some are considered legitimate. Others not to be raised in polite society. A third kind seem to make no sense at all. If you raise these, you risk being thought a fiend or impossibly vain. The distinction between the *vernacular domain* and the *shadow economy* is of that kind. With this essay I want to draw this distinction into the realm of permissible discussion.

During the seventies social and economic analysis broadened. First, environmental constraints became obvious and were increasingly defined. Second, the black market in labor and produce was recognized in its full importance to modern economies. Transactions that evade the tax law, that are done by scabs, that are performed without licence or paid for in kind rather than in cash were progressively included into their plans by policy makers. Nearly half of all legitimate economic transactions in Italy, Poland or India are illegal – 'black market'. But thirdly, economists have increasingly invaded the informal sector to map it out for colonization by policy makers. And by doing so, they have begun to eat pork.

In this essay I want to distinguish economic pork from vernacular begonias. Only indirectly am I concerned with the legitimacy of serving economic pork, black market goods and legitimate staples on one single menu.

Economists can only deal with realms they can measure. For forays into the non-marketed, they need new sticks. To function where money is not the currency, the concepts must be *sui generis*. But to avoid splitting their science, the new tools must be consistent with the old. Pigou defined the shadow price as one such tool. It is the money needed to substitute through a good or service something which is now done without pay. The unpaid and, perhaps, even the priceless thus become consistent with the realm of commodities, enter a domain that can be operationalized, managed and bureaucratically developed. The unpaid becomes part of a shadow economy and is related to the wares in supermarkets, classrooms, and medical clinics as the wave to the particle – electrons are not intelligible unless one examines both theories.

Close analysis reveals that this shadow economy mirrors the formal economy. The two fields are in synergy, together constituting one whole. The shadow economy developed a complete range of parallel activities, following the brightly illuminated realm where labor, prices, needs and markets were increasingly managed as industrial production increased. Thus we see that the housework of a modern woman is as radically new as the wage labor of her husband; the replacement of home-cooked food by restaurant delivery is as new as the definition of most basic needs in terms which correspond to the outputs of modern institutions.

I argue elsewhere that the new competence of some economists, enabling them to analyze this shady area, is more than an expansion of their conventional economic analysis – it is the discovery of new land which, like the industrial market, emerged for the first time in history only during the last two centuries. I feel sorrow for such economists who do not understand what they are doing. Their destiny is as sad as that of Columbus. With the compass, the new caravel designed to follow the route the compass opened, and his own flair as a mariner, he was able to hit on unexpected land. But he died, unaware that he had chanced on a hemisphere, firmly attached to the belief that he had reached the Indies.

In an industrial world, the realm of shadow economics is comparable to the hidden side of the moon, also being explored for the first time. And the whole of this *industrial* reality is in turn complementary to a substantive domain which I call the *vernacular* reality, the domain of subsistence.

In terms of twentieth century classical economics, both the shadow economy and the vernacular domain are outside the market, both are unpaid. Therefore, both are confused in the so-called informal sector. And both are indistinctly viewed as contributions to 'social reproduction'. But what is most confusing in the analysis is the fact that the unpaid complement of wage labor which, in its structure, is characteristic of industrial societies only, is often completely misunderstood as the survival of subsistence activities, which are characteristic of the *vernacular* societies and which may continue to exist in an industrial society.

Certain changes can now be discerned. The distinction between the market economy and its shadow weakens. The substitution of commodities for subsistence activities is not necessarily experienced as progress. Women ask whether the unearned consumption which accompanies homemaking is a privilege or whether they are actually forced into degrading work by the prevailing patterns of compulsory consumption. Students ask if they are in school to learn or to collaborate in their own stupefaction. Increasingly, the toil of consumption overshadows the relief consumption promised. The choice between labor-intensive consumption, perhaps less inhuman, less destructive and better organized, and modern forms of subsistence is personally known to more and more people. The choice corresponds to the difference between an expanding shadow economy and the recovery of the vernacular domain. But it is precisely this choice which is the most resistant blind spot of economics, as unpalatable as dog or clay. Perhaps the most unlikely candidate can help dispel some of the darkness. I propose to throw light on this issue through an examination of *everyday speech*. I shall proceed by contrasting the economic nature of this speech in industrial society with its counterpart in preindustrial epochs. As I shall show, the distinction finds its origin in a little-known event which occurred at the end of the fifteenth century in Spain.

Early on August 3, 1492, Christopher Columbus sailed from Palos. The neighboring and much more important Cadíz was congested that year – it was the one port from which Jews were allowed to leave. Granada had been reconquered, and Jewish

service was no longer needed for a struggle with Islam. Columbus headed for Cipangu, the name for Cathay (China) during
the short reign of the long dead Tamerlane. He had calculated
the earth's degree as equivalent to forty-five miles. This would
place Eastern Asia 2,400 miles west of the Canaries, somewhere
close to the Antilles in the Saragossa Sea. He had reduced the
ocean to the range of the ships he could master. Columbus had
on board an Arabic interpreter to enable him to speak to the
great Khan. He set out to discover a route, not new land, not a
new hemisphere.

His project, however, was quite unreasonable. No learned
man of the early Renaissance doubted that the earth was a
globe – some believing that it rested at the center of the universe,
and some that it whirled in its sphere. But not since Eratosthenes had anyone underestimated its size as badly as Columbus.
In 255, Eratosthenes of Cyrene measured the distance from the
great library that he directed in Alexandria to Syene (now the
site of the Aswan Dam) as 500 miles. He measured the distance
using the camel caravan's remarkably steady gait from sunrise
to sunset as his 'rod'. He had observed that on the day of the
summer solstice, the rays of the sun fell vertically at Syene, and
seven degrees off the vertical at Alexandria. From this he calculated the earth's circumference to about 5 percent of its real
dimension.

When Columbus sought Queen Isabella's support for his ven-
ture, she asked Talavera, the sage, to evaluate its feasibility. An
expert commission reported that the West-to-the-Orient project
lacked a firm foundation. Educated authorities believed its goal
to be uncertain or impossible. The proposed voyage would
require three years; it was doubtful that even the newest kind of
ship, a caravel – designed for distant explorations – could ever
return. The oceans were neither as small nor as navigable as
Columbus supposed. And it was hardly likely that God would
have allowed any uninhabited lands of real value to be con-
cealed from his people for so many centuries. Initially, then, the
Queen rejected Columbus; reason and bureaucratic expertise
supported her. Later, swayed by zealous Franciscan friars, she
retracted her earlier decision and signed her 'stipulations' with
Columbus. She, who had driven Islam from Europe, could not
refuse her Admiral who wanted to plant the Cross beyond the

Ocean Seas. And, as we shall see, the decision for colonial conquest overseas implied the challenge of a new war at home – the invasion of her own people's vernacular domain, the opening of a five-century war against vernacular subsistence, the ravages of which we now begin to fathom.

For five weeks Columbus sailed well known waters. He put in at the Canary Islands to repair the rudder of the Pinta, to replace the lateen sail of the Niña, and to pursue a mysterious affair with Dona Beatriz de Peraza. Only on September 10, two days out of the Canaries, he picked up the Easterlies, tradewinds on which he chanced, and which carried him rapidly across the ocean. In October, he came upon land that neither he nor the Queen's counselors had expected. In his diary entry for October 13, 1492, he beautifully described the song of the nightingale that welcomed him on Santo Domingo, though such birds never lived there. Columbus was and remained *gran maribero y mediocre cosmógrafo*. To the end of his life he remained convinced of having found what he had sought – a Spanish nightingale on the shores of China.

Let me now move from the reasonably well known to the unreasonably overlooked – from Columbus, immediately associated with 1492, to Elio Antonio de Nebrija, outside of Spain almost forgotten. During the time Columbus cruised southwest through recognizable Portuguese waters and harbors, in Spain the fundamental engineering of a new social reality was proposed to the Queen. While Columbus sailed for foreign lands to seek the familiar – gold, subjects, nightingales – in Spain Nebrija advocates the reduction of the Queen's subjects to an entirely new type of dependence. He presents her with a new weapon, grammar, to be wielded by a new kind of mercenary, the *letrado*.

I was deeply moved when I felt Nebrija's *Gramatica Castellana* in my hands – a quarto volume of five signatures set in Gothic letters. The epigraphy is printed in red, and a blank page precedes the Introduction:

A la muy alta e assi esclarecida princesa dona Isabela la tercera deste nombre Reina i senora natural de espana e las islas de nuestro mar. Comienza la gramática que nuevamenta hizo el maestro Antonio de

Nebrixa sobre la lengua castellana, e pone primero el prólogo. Léelo en buena hora.

The Conqueror of Granada receives a petition, similar to many others. But unlike the request of Columbus, who wanted resources to establish a new route to the China of Marco Polo, that of Nebrija urges the Queen to invade a new domain at home. He offers Isabella a tool to colonize the language spoken by her own subjects; he wants her to replace the people's speech by the imposition of the queen's *lengua* – *her* language, *her* tongue.

I shall translate and comment on sections of the six-page introduction to Nebrija's grammar. Remember, then, that the colophon of the *Gramática Castellana* notes that it came off the press in Salamanca on the 18th of August, just fifteen days after Columbus had sailed.

> My Illustrious Queen. Whenever I ponder over the tokens of the past that have been preserved in writing, I am forced to the very same conclusion. Language has always been the consort of empire, and forever shall remain its mate. Together they come into being, together they grow and flower, and together they decline.

To understand what *la lengua*, 'language', meant for Nebrija, it is necessary to know who he was. Antonio Martinez de la Cala, *converso*, descendant of Jewish converts, had decided at the age of nineteen that Latin, at least on the Iberian peninsula, had become so corrupted that one could say it had died of neglect. Thus Spain was left without a language (*una lengua*) worthy of the name. The *languages* of Scripture – Greek, Latin, Hebrew – clearly were something other than the *speech of the people*. Nebrija then went to Italy where, in his opinion, Latin was least corrupted. When he returned to Spain, his contemporary, Hernán Nunez, wrote that it was like Orpheus bringing Euridice back from Hades. During the next twenty years, Nebrija dedicated himself to the renewal of classical grammar and rhetoric. The first full book printed in Salamanca was his Latin grammar (1482).

When he reached his forties and began to age – as he puts it – he discovered that he could make a language out of the speech forms he daily encountered in Spain – to engineer, to synthesize chemically, a language. He then wrote his Spanish grammar, the first in any modern European tongue. The *converso* uses his classical formation to extend the juridic category of *consuetudo hispaniae* to the realm of language. Throughout the Iberian peninsula, crowds speaking various languages gather for pogroms against the Jewish outsider at the very moment when the cosmopolitan *converso* offers his services to the Crown – the creation of one language suitable for use wherever the sword could carry it.

Nebrija created two rule books, both at the service of the Queen's regime. First, he wrote a grammar. Now grammars were not new. The most perfect of them, unknown to Nebrija, was already two thousand years old – Panini's grammar of Sanskrit. This was an attempt to describe a dead language, to be taught only to a very few. This is the goal pursued by Prakrit grammarians in India, and Latin or Greek grammarians in the West. Nebrija's work, however, was written as a tool for conquest abroad and a weapon to suppress untutored speech at home.

While he worked on his grammar, Nebrija also wrote a dictionary that, to this day, remains the single best source of Old Spanish. The two attempts made in our lifetime to supersede him both failed. Gili Gaya's *Tesauro Lexicográfico*, begun in 1947, foundered on the letter E, and R. S. Boggs (*Tentative Dictionary of Medieval Spanish*) remains, since 1946, an often copied draft. Nebrija's dictionary appeared the year after his grammar, and already contained evidence of the New World – the first Americanism, *canoa* (canoe), appeared.

Now note what Nebrija thinks about Castilian.

Castilian went through its infancy at the time of the judges . . . it waxed in strength under Alfonso the Learned. It was he who collected law and history books in Greek and Latin and had them translated.

Indeed, Alfonso (1221–1284) was the first European monarch to use the vulgar or vernacular tongue of the scribes as his chancery language. His intent was to demonstrate that he was not one of the Latin kings. Like a caliph, he ordered his courtiers to undertake pilgrimages through Muslim and Christian books, and transform them into treasures that, because of their very language, would be a valuable inheritance to leave his kingdom. Incidentally, most of his translators were Jews from Toledo. And these Jews – whose own language was Old Castilian – preferred to translate the oriental languages into the vernacular rather than into Latin, the sacred language of the Church.

Nebrija points out to the Queen that Alfonso had left solid tokens of Old Spanish; in addition, he had worked toward the transformation of vernacular speech into language proper through using it to make laws, to record history, and to translate from the classics. He continues:

This our language followed our soldiers whom we sent abroad to rule. It spread to Aragon, to Navarra, even to Italy . . . the scattered bits and pieces of Spain were thus gathered and joined into one single kingdom.

Nebrija here reminds the Queen of the new pact possible between sword and book. He proposes a covenant between two spheres, both within the secular realm of the Crown, a covenant distinct from the medieval pact between Emperor and Pope, which had been a covenant bridging the secular and the sacred. He proposes a pact, not of sword and cloth – each sovereign in its own sphere – but of sword and expertise, encompassing the engine of conquest abroad and a system of scientific control of diversity within the entire kingdom. And he knows well whom he addresses: the wife of Ferdinand of Aragon, a woman he once praised as the most enlightened of all men (sic). He is aware that she reads Cicero, Seneca, and Livy in the original for her own pleasure; and that she possesses a sensibility that unites the physical and spiritual into what she herself called 'good taste'. Indeed, historians claim that she is the first to use this expression. Together with Ferdinand, she was trying to give shape to the chaotic Castile they had inherited; together they were creating Renaissance institutions of government, institutions apt for the making of a modern state, and yet, something better than a nation of lawyers. Nebrija calls to their minds a concept that, to this day, is powerful in Spanish – *armas y letras*. He speaks about the marriage of empire and language, addressing the sovereign who had just recently – and for a painfully short time – seized from the Church the Inquisition, in order to use it as a secular instrument of royal power. The monarchy used it to gain economic control of the grandees, and to replace noblemen by the *letrados* of Nebrija on the governing councils of the kingdom. This was the monarchy that transformed the older advisory bodies into bureaucratic organizations of civil servants, institutions fit only for the execution of royal policies. These secretaries or ministries of 'experts', under the court ceremonial of the Hapsburgs, were later assigned a ritual role in processions and receptions incomparable to any other secular bureaucracy since the times of Byzantium.

Very astutely, Nebrija's argument reminds the Queen that a new union of *armas y letras*, complementary to that of church and state, was essential to gather and join the scattered pieces of Spain into a single absolute kingdom.

This unified and sovereign body will be of such shape and inner cohesion that centuries will be unable to undo it. Now that the Church has been purified, and we are thus reconciled to God [does he think of the work of his contemporary, Torquemade?], now that the enemies of the Faith have been subdued by our arms [he refers to the apogee of the *Reconquista*] now that just laws are being enforced, enabling all of us to live as equals [perhaps having in mind the *Hermandades*], what else remains but the flowering of the peaceful arts. And among the arts, foremost are those of language, which sets us apart from wild animals; language, which is the unique distinction of man, the means for the kind of understanding which can be surpassed only by contemplation.

In this passage we distinctly hear the appeal of the humanist to the prince, requesting him to defend the realm of civilized Christians against the domain of the wild. The wild man's inability to speak is part of the Wild Man Myth whenever we meet him during the Middle Ages . . . in a morally ordered world, to be wild is to be incoherent mute . . . sinful and accursed. Formerly, the heathen was to be brought into the fold through baptism; henceforth, through language. Language now needs tutors.

Nebrija then points out:

So far, this our language has been left loose and unruly and, therefore, in just a few centuries this language has changed beyond recognition. If we were to compare what we speak today with the language spoken five hundred years ago, we would notice a difference and a diversity that could not be any greater if these were two alien tongues.

Nebrija describes the evolution and extension of vernacular tongues, of the *lengua vulgar*, through time. He refers to the untutored speech of Castile – different from that of Aragon and Navarra, regions where soldiers had recently introduced Castilian – but a speech also different from the older Castilian into which Alfonso's monks and Jews had translated the Greek classics from their Arabic versions. In the fifteenth century people felt and lived their languages otherwise than we do today. The study of Columbus' language made by Menendez Pidal helps us to understand this. Columbus, originally a cloth merchant from Genoa, had as his first language Genovese, a dialect still standardized today. He learned to write business letters in Latin of a quite barbarous variety. After being shipwrecked in Portugal, he married a Portuguese and probably forgot most of his Italian. He spoke, but never wrote, a word of Portuguese. During his nine years in Lisbon, he took up writing in Spanish. But he never used his brilliant mind to learn Spanish well and always wrote it in a hybrid, Portuguese-mannered style. His Spanish is not Castilian but is rich in simple words picked up all over the peninsula. In spite of some syntactical monstrosities, he handles this language in a lively, expressive, and precise fashion. Columbus, then, wrote in two languages he did not speak, and spoke several. None of this seems to have been problematic for his contemporaries. However, it is also true that none of these were languages in the eyes of Nebrija.

Continuing to develop his petition, he introduces *the* crucial element of his argument: *La lengua suelta y fuera de regla,* the un-bound and ungoverned speech in which people actually live and manage their lives, has become a challenge to the Crown. He now interprets an unproblematic historical fact as a problem for the architects of a new kind of polity – the modern state.

> Your Majesty, it has been my constant desire to see our nation become great, and to provide the men of my tongue with books worthy of their leisure. Presently, they waste their time on novels and fancy stories full of lies.

Nebrija proposes to regularize language to stop people from wasting time on frivolous reading, *"quando la emprenta aun no informaba la lengua de los libros."* And Nebrija is not the only late fifteenth-century person concerned with the 'waste' of leisure time made possible through the inventions of paper and mov-able type. Ignatius of Loyola, twenty-nine years later, while convalescing in Pamplona with a leg shattered by a cannonball, came to believe that he had disastrously wasted his youth. At thirty, he looked back on his life as one filled with "the vanities of the world . . .", whose leisure had included the reading of vernacular trash.

Nebrija argues for standardizing a living language for the benefit of its printed form. This argument is also made in our generation, but the end now is different. Our contemporaries believe that standardized language is a necessary condition to teach people to read, indispensable for the distribution of printed books. The argument in 1492 is the opposite: Nebrija is upset because people who speak in dozens of distinct vernacular tongues have become the victims of a reading epidemic. They waste their leisure, throwing away their time on books that circulate outside of any possible bureaucratic control. A manu-script was so precious and rare that authorities could often sup-press the work of an author by literally seizing *all* the copies.

Manuscripts could sometimes be extirpated by the roots. Not so books. Even with the small editions of two hundred to less than a thousand copies – typical for the first generation of print – it would never be possible to confiscate an entire run. Printed books called for the exercise of censorship through an *Index of Forbidden Books*. Books could only be proscribed, not destroyed. But Nebrija's proposal appeared more than fifty years before the *Index* was published in 1559. And he wishes to achieve control over the printed word on a much deeper level than what the Church later attempted through proscription. He wants to re-place the people's vernacular by the grammarian's language. The humanist proposes the standardization of colloquial language to remove the new technology of printing from the verna-cular domain – to prevent people from printing and reading in the various languages that, up to that time, they had only spoken. By this monopoly over an official and taught language, he proposes to suppress wild, untaught vernacular reading.

To grasp the full significance of Nebrija's argument – the argu-ment that compulsory education in a standardized national tongue is necessary to stop people from wanton reading that gives them an easy pleasure – one must remember the status of print at that time. Nebrija was born before the appearance of movable type. He was thirteen when the first movable stock came into use. His conscious adult life coincides with the Incu-nabula. When printing was in its twenty-fifth year, he published his Latin grammar; when it was in its thirty-fifth year, his Spanish grammar. Nebrija could recall the time before print, as I can the time before television. Nebrija's text, on which I am commenting, was by coincidence published the year Thomas Caxton died. And Caxton's work itself furthers our understand-ing of the *vernacular* book.

Thomas Caxton was an English cloth merchant living in the Netherlands. He took up translating, and then apprenticed him-self to a printer. After publishing a few books in English, he took his press to England in 1476. By the time he died (1491), he had published forty translations into English, and nearly everything available in English vernacular literature, with the notable exception of William Langland's *Piers Plowman*. I have often wondered if he left this important work off his list because of the challenge it might present to one of his best sellers – *The Art and Crafte to Knowe Well to Dye*. This volume of his Westminster Press belongs to the first series of self-help books. Whatever would train for a society well informed and well mannered, whatever would lead to behavior gentle and devout, was gathered in small folios and quartos of neat Gothic print – instructions on everything from manipulating a knife to conducting a conversation, from the art of weeping to the art of playing chess to that of dying. Before 1500, no less than 100 editions of this last book had appeared. It is a self-instruction manual showing one how to prepare to die with dignity and without the intervention of physician or clergy.

Four categories of books first appeared in the peoples' languages: vernacular, native literature; translations from French and Latin; devotional books; and already there were the how-to-do-it manuals that made teachers unnecessary. Printed books in Latin were of a different sort, comprising textbooks, rituals, and lawbooks – books at the service of professional clergymen and teachers. From the very beginning, printed books were of two kinds: those which readers independently chose for their pleasure, and those professionally prescribed for the reader's own good. It is estimated that before 1500, more than seventeen hundred presses in almost three hundred European towns had produced one or more books. Almost forty thousand editions were published during the fifteenth century, comprising somewhere between fifteen and twenty million copies. About one third of these were published in the various vernacular languages of Europe. This portion of printed books is the source of Nebrija's concern.

To appreciate more fully his worry about the freedom to read, one must remember that reading in his time was not silent. Silent reading is a recent invention. Augustine was already a great author and the Bishop of Hippo when he found that it could be done. In his *Confessions*, he describes the discovery. During the night, charity forbade him to disturb his fellow monks with noises he made while reading. But curiosity impelled him to pick up a book. So, he learned to read in silence, an art that he had observed in only one man, his teacher, Ambrose of Milan. Ambrose practiced the art of silent reading because otherwise people would have gathered around him and would have interrupted him with their queries on the text. Loud reading was the link between classical learning and popular culture.

Habitual reading in a loud voice produces social effects. It is an extraordinarily effective way of teaching the art to those who look over the reader's shoulder; rather than being confined to a sublime or sublimated form of self-satisfaction, it promotes community intercourse; it actively leads to common digestion of and comment on the passages read. In most of the languages of India, the verb that translates into 'reading' has a meaning close to 'sounding'. The same verb characterizes the book and the sound of the vina. To read and to play a musical instrument are perceived as parallel activities. The current, simpleminded, internationally accepted definition of literacy obscures an alternate approach to book, print, and reading. If reading were conceived primarily as a social activity as, for example, competence in playing the guitar, fewer readers could mean a much broader access to books and literature.

Reading aloud was common in Europe before Nebrija's time. Print multiplied and spread opportunities for this infectious reading in an epidemic manner. Further, the line between literate and illiterate was different from what we recognize now. Literate was he who had been taught Latin. The great mass of people, thoroughly conversant with the vernacular literature of their region, either did not know how to read and write, had picked it up on their own, had been instructed as accountants, had left the clergy or, even if they knew it, hardly used their Latin. This held true for the poor and for many nobles, especially women. And we sometimes forget that even today the rich, many professionals, and high-level bureaucrats have assistants report a verbal digest of documents and information, while they call on secretaries to write what they dictate.

To the Queen, Nebrija's proposed enterprise must have seemed even more improbable than Columbus' project. But, ultimately, it turned out to be more fundamental than the New World for the rise of the Hapsburg Empire. Nebrija clearly showed the way to prevent the free and anarchic development

of printing technology, and laid down exactly how to transform
it into the evolving national state's instrument of bureaucratic
control.

Today, we generally act on the assumption that books could
not be printed and would not be read in any number if they
were written in a vernacular language free from the constraints
of an official grammar. Equally, we assume that people could
not learn to read and write their own tongue unless they are
taught in the same manner as students were traditionally taught
Latin. Let us listen again to Nebrija.

> By means of my grammar, they shall learn artificial Castilian,
> not difficult to do, since it is built up on the base of a language
> they know; and, then, Latin will come easily . . .

Nebrija already considers the vernacular as a raw material from
which his Castilian art can be produced, a resource to be mined,
not unlike the Brazilwood and human chattel that, Columbus
sadly concluded, were the only resources of value or importance
in Cuba.

Nebrija does not seek to teach grammar that people learn to
read. Rather, he implores Isabella to give him the power and
authority to stem the anarchic spread of reading by the use of
his grammar.

> Presently, they waste their leisure on novels and fancy stories
> full of lies. I have decided, therefore, that my most urgent
> task is to transform Castilian speech into an artifact so that
> whatever henceforth shall be written in this language may be
> of one standard tenor.

Nebrija frankly states what he wants to do and even provides
the outline of his incredible project. He deliberately turns the
mate of empire into its slave. Here the first modern language
expert advises the Crown on the way to make, out of a people's
speech and lives, tools that befit the state and its pursuits.
Nebrija's grammar is conceived by him as a pillar of the nation
state. Through it, the state is seen, from its very beginning, as an

aggressively productive agency. The new state takes from people the words on which they subsist, and transforms them into the standardized language which henceforth they are compelled to use, each one at the level of education that has been institutionally imputed to him. Henceforth, people will have to rely on the language they receive from above, rather than to develop a tongue in common with one another. The switch from the vernacular to an officially taught mother tongue is perhaps the most significant – and, therefore, least researched – event in the coming of a commodity-intensive society. The radical change from the vernacular to taught language foreshadows the switch from breast to bottle, from subsistence to welfare, from production for use to production for market, from expectations divided between state and church to a world where the Church is marginal, religion is privatized, and the state assumes the maternal functions heretofore claimed only by the Church. Formerly, there had been no salvation outside the Church; now, there would be no reading, no writing – if possible no speaking – outside the educational sphere. People would have to be reborn out of the monarch's womb and be nourished at her breast. Both the citizen of the modern state and his state-provided language come into being for the first time – both are without precedent anywhere in history.

But dependence on a formal, bureaucratic institution to obtain for every individual a service that is as necessary as breast milk for human subsistence, while radically new and without parallel outside of Europe, was not a break with Europe's past. Rather, this was a logical step forward – a process first legitimated in the Christian Church that evolved into an accepted and expected temporal function of the secular state. Institutional maternity has a unique European history since the third century. In this sense, it is indeed true that Europe is the Church and the Church is Europe. Nebrija and universal education in the modern state cannot be understood without a close knowledge of the Church, insofar as this institution is represented as a mother.

From the very earliest days, the Church is called 'mother'. Marcion the Gnostic uses this designation in 144. At first, the community of the faithful is meant to be mother to the new

members whom communion, that is, the fact of celebrating
community, engenders. Soon, however, the Church becomes a
mother outside of whose bosom it is hardly worthwhile to be
called human or to be alive. But the origins of the Church's self-
understanding as mother have been little researched. One can
often find comments about the role of mother goddesses in the
various religions scattered throughout the Roman Empire at the
time Christianity began to spread. But the fact that no previous
community had ever been called mother has yet to be noticed
and studied. We know that the image of the Church as mother
comes from Syria, and that it flourished in the third century in
North Africa. On a beautiful mosaic near Tripoli, where the
claim is first expressed, both the invisible community and the
visible building are represented as mother. And Rome is the
last place where the metaphor is applied to the Church. The
female personification of an institution did not fit the Roman
style; the idea is first taken up only late in the fourth century in
a poem by Pope Damasus.

This early Christian notion of the Church as mother has no
historical precedent. No direct gnostic or pagan influence, nor
any direct relationship to the Roman mother cult has thus far
been proven. The description of the Church's maternity is, however, quite explicit. The Church conceives, bears, and gives
birth to her sons and daughters. She may have a miscarriage.
She raises her children to her breast to nourish them with the
milk of faith. In this early period, the institutional trait is clearly
present, but the maternal authority exercised by the Church
through her bishops and the ritual treatment of the Church
building as a female entity are still balanced by the insistence on
the motherly quality of God's love, and of the mutual love of
His children in baptism. Later, the image of the Church as a
prototype of the authoritarian and possessive mother becomes
dominant in the Middle Ages. The popes then insist on an
understanding of the Church as *Mater*, *Magistra*, and *Domina* –
mother, authoritative teacher, sovereign. Thus Gregory VII
(1073–1085) names her in the struggle with the emperor Henry
IV.

Nebrija's introduction is addressed to a Queen intent on
building a modern state. And his argument implies that, institutionally, the state must now assume the universally maternal

functions heretofore claimed only by the Church. *Educatio*, as a function first institutionalized at the bosom of Mother Church, becomes a function of the Crown in the process of the modern state's formation.

Educatio prolis is a term that in Latin grammar calls for a female subject. It designates the feeding and nurturing in which mothers engage, be they bitch, sow, or woman. Among humans only women educate. And they educate only infants, which etymologically means those who are yet without speech. To educate has etymologically nothing to do with 'drawing out' as pedagogical folklore would have it. Pestalozzi should have heeded Cicero: educit obstetrix – educat nutrix: the midwife draws – the nurse nurtures, because men do neither in Latin They engage in *docentia* (teaching) and *instructio* (instruction). The first men who attributed to themselves educational functions were early bishops who led their flocks to the *alma ubera* (milk-brimming breasts) of Mother Church from which they were never to be weaned. This is why they, like their secular successors, call the faithful *alumni* – which means sucklings or suckers, and nothing else. It is this transfer of woman's functions to specialized institutional spheres governed by clergies that Nebrija helped to bring about. In the process the state acquired the function of a many-uddered provider of distinct forms of sustenance, each corresponding to a separate basic need, and each guarded and managed by the clergy, always male in the higher reaches of the hierarchy.

Actually, when Nebrija proposes to transform Castilian into an artifact, as necessary for the Queen's subjects as faith for the Christian, he appeals to the hermetic tradition. In the language of his time, the two words he uses – *reducir* and *artificio* – have both an ordinary and a technical meaning. In the latter case, they belong to the language of alchemy.

According to Nebrija's own dictionary, *reducir* in fifteenth-century Spanish means 'to change', 'to bring into obeisance', and 'to civilize'. In this last sense, the Jesuits later understood the *Reducciones de Paraguay*. In addition, *reductio* – throughout the fifteenth and sixteenth centuries – means one of the seven stages by which ordinary elements of nature are transmuted into the philosopher's stone, into the panacea that, by touch, turns everything into gold. Here, *reductio* designates the fourth of seven grades of sublimation. It designates the crucial test that must be passed by grey matter to be promoted from the primary to the secondary grades of enlightenment. In the first four grades, raw nature is successively liquefied, purified, and evaporated. In the fourth grade, that of *reductio*, it is nourished on philosopher's milk. If it takes to this substance, which will occur only if the first three processes have completely voided its unruly and raw nature, the chrysosperm, the sperm of gold hidden in its depth, can be brought forth. This is *educatio*. During the following three stages, the alchemist can coagulate his *alumnus* – the substance he has fed with his milk – into the philosopher's stone. The precise language used here is a bit posterior to Nebrija. It is taken almost literally from Paracelsus, another man born within a year of the publication of the *Gramatica Castellana*.

Now let us return to the text. Nebrija develops his argument:

I have decided to transform Castilian into an artifact so that whatever shall be written henceforth in this language shall be of one standard tenor, one coinage that can outlast the times. Greek and Latin have been governed by art, and thus have kept their uniformity throughout the ages. Unless the like of this be done for our language, in vain Your Majesty's chroniclers . . . shall praise your deeds. Your labor will not last more than a few years, and we shall continue to feed on Castilian translations of foreign tales about our own kings. Either your feats will fade with the language or they will roam among aliens abroad, homeless, without a dwelling in which they can settle.

The Roman Empire could be governed through the Latin of its élite. But the traditional, separate élite language used in former empires for keeping records, maintaining international relations, and advancing learning – like Persian, Arabic, Latin, or Frankish – is insufficient to realize the aspirations of nationalistic monarchies. The modern European state cannot function in the world of the vernacular. The new national state needs an *artificio*, unlike the perennial Latin of diplomacy and the perishable Castilian of Alfonso the Learned. This kind of polity requires a standard language understood by all those subject to its laws and for whom the tales written at the monarch's behest (that is, propaganda) are destined.

However, Nebrija does not suggest that Latin be abandoned. On the contrary, the neo-Latin renaissance in Spain owed its existence largely to his grammar, dictionary, and textbooks. But his important innovation was to lay the foundation for a linguistic ideal without precedent: the creation of a society in which the universal ruler's bureaucrats, soldiers, merchants, and peasants all pretend to speak one language, a language the poor are presumed to understand and to obey. Nebrija established the notion of a kind of ordinary language that itself is sufficient to place each man in his assigned place on the pyramid that education in a mother tongue necessarily constructs. In his argument, he insists that Isabella's claim to historical fame depends on forging a language of propaganda – universal and fixed like Latin, yet capable of penetrating every village and farm, to reduce subjects into modern citizens.

How times had changed since Dante! For Dante, a language that had to be learned, to be spoken according to a grammar, was inevitably a dead tongue. For him, such a language was fit only for schoolmen, whom he cynically called *inventores grammaticae facultatis*. What for Dante was dead and useless, Nebrija recommends as a tool. One was interested in vital exchange, the other in universal conquest, in a language that by rule would coin words as incorruptible as the stones of a palace:

> Your Majesty, I want to lay the foundations for the dwelling in which your fame can settle. I want to do for our language what Zeno has done for Greek, and Crates for Latin. I do not doubt that their betters have come to succeed them. But the fact that their pupils have improved on them does not detract from their or, I should say, from our glory – to be the inventors of a necessary craft just when the time for such invention was ripe. Trust me, Your Majesty, no craft has ever arrived more timely than grammar for the Castilian tongue at this time.

The expert is always in a hurry, but his belief in progress gives him the language of humility. The academic adventurer pushes his government to adopt his idea now, under threat of failure to achieve its imperial designs. This is the time!

Our language has indeed just now reached a height from which we must fear more that we sink, than we can ever hope to rise.

Nebrija's last paragraph in the introduction exudes eloquence. Evidently the teacher of rhetoric knew what he taught. Nebrija has explained his project; given the Queen logical reasons to accept it; frightened her with what would happen if she were not to heed him; now, finally, like Columbus, he appeals to her sense of a manifest destiny.

Now, Your Majesty, let me come to the last advantage that you shall gain from my grammar. For the purpose, recall the time when I presented you with a draft of this book earlier this year in Salamanca. At this time, you asked me what end such grammar could possibly serve. Upon this, the Bishop of Avila interrupted to answer in my stead. What he said was this: "Soon Your Majesty will have placed her yoke upon many barbarians who speak outlandish tongues. By this, your victory, these people shall stand in a new need; the need for the laws the victor owes to the vanquished, and the need for the language we shall bring with us." My grammar shall serve to impart to them the Castilian tongue, as we have used grammar to teach Latin to our young.

We can attempt a reconstruction of what happened at Salamanca when Nebrija handed the Queen a draft of his forthcoming book. The Queen praised the humanist for having provided the Castilian tongue with what had been reserved to the languages of Scripture – Hebrew, Greek, and Latin. (It is surprising and significant that the *converso*, in the year of Granada, does not mention the Arabic of the Koran!) But while Isabella was able to grasp the achievement of her *letrado* – the description of a living tongue as rules of grammar – she was unable to see any practical purpose in such an undertaking. For her, grammar was an instrument designed solely for use by teachers. She believed, however, that the vernacular simply could not be taught. In her royal view of linguistics, every subject of her many kingdoms was so made by nature that during his lifetime he would reach perfect dominion over his tongue *on his own*. In this version of 'majestic linguistics', the vernacular is the subject's domain. By the very nature of things, the vernacular is beyond the reach of the Spanish Monarch's authority. But the ruler forging the nation state is unable to see the logic inherent in the project. Isabella's initial rejection underscores the originality of Nebrija's proposal.

This discussion of Nebrija's draft about the need for instruction to speak one's mother tongue must have taken place in the months around March, 1492, the same time Columbus argued his project with the Queen. At first, Isabella refused Columbus on the advice of technical counsel – he had miscalculated the circumference of the globe. But Nebrija's proposal she rejected out of a different motive: from royal respect for the autonomy of her subject's tongues. This respect of the Crown for the juridic autonomy of each village, of the *fuero del pueblo*, the judgment by peers, was perceived by people and sovereign as the fundamental freedom of Christians engaged in the reconquest of Spain. Nebrija argues against this traditional and typically Iberic prejudice of Isabella – the notion that the Crown cannot encroach on the variety of customs in the kingdoms – and calls up the image of a new, universal mission for a *modern* Crown.

Ultimately, Columbus won out because his Franciscan friends presented him to the Queen as a man driven by God to serve her mystical mission. Nebrija proceeds in the same fashion. First, he argues that the vernacular must be replaced by an *artificio* to give the monarch's power increased range and duration; then, to cultivate the arts by decision of the court; also, to guard the established order against the threat presented by wanton reading and printing. But he concludes his petition with an appeal to "the Grace of Granada" – the Queen's destiny, not just to conquer, but to civilize the whole world.

Both Columbus and Nebrija offer their services to a new kind of empire builder. But Columbus proposes only to use the recently created caravels to the limit of their range for the expansion of royal power in what would become New Spain. Nebrija is more basic – he argues the use of his grammar for the expansion of the Queen's power in a totally new sphere: state control over the kind of sustenance on which people may draw every day. In effect, Nebrija drafts the declaration of war against subsistence which the new state was organizing to fight. He intends to replace the vernacular with taught mother tongue – the first invented part of universal education.

III

THE WAR AGAINST
SUBSISTENCE

HISTORIANS have chosen Columbus' voyage from Palos as a date convenient for marking the transition from the Middle Ages to modern times, a point useful for changing editors of textbooks. But the world of Ptolemy did not become the world of Mercator in one year, nor did the world of the vernacular become the age of education overnight. Rather, traditional cosmography was gradually adjusted in the light of widening experience. Columbus was followed by Cortéz, Copernicus by Kepler, Nebrija by Comenius. Unlike personal insight, the change in world view that generated our dependence on goods and services took 500 years.

How often the hand of the clock advances depends on the language of the ciphers on the quadrant. The Chinese speak of five stages in sprouting, and dawn approaches in seven steps for the Arabs. If I were to describe the evolution of *homo economicus* from Mandeville to Marx or Galbraith, I would come to a different view of epochs than if I had a mind to outline the stages in which the ideology of *homo educandus* developed from Nebrija through Radke to Comenius. And again, within this same paradigm, a different set of turning points would best describe the decay of untutored learning and the route toward the inescapable miseducation that educational institutions necessarily dispense.

It took a good decade to recognize that Columbus had found a new hemisphere, not just a new route. It took much longer to invent the concept 'New World' for the continent whose existence he had denied.

A full century and a half separated the claim of Nebrija – in the Queen's service he *had* to teach all her subjects to speak – and the claim of John Amos Comenius – the possession of a method by which an army of schoolteachers would teach everybody everything perfectly.

By the time of Comenius (1592–1670), the ruling groups of both the Old and New Worlds were deeply convinced of the need for such a method. An incident in the history of Harvard College aptly illustrates the point. On the one hundred and fiftieth birthday of Nebrija's grammar, John Winthrop, Jr. was on his way to Europe searching for a theologian and educator to accept the presidency of Harvard. One of the first persons he approached was the Czech Comenius, leader and last bishop of the Moravian Church. Winthrop found him in London, where he was organizing the Royal Society and advising the government on public schools. In *Magna Didactica, vel Ars Omnibus Omnia Omnino Docendi*, Comenius had succinctly defined the goals of his profession. Education begins in the womb and does not end until death. Whatever is worth knowing is worth teaching by a special method appropriate to the subject. The preferred world is the one so organized that it functions as a school for all. Only if learning is the result of teaching can individuals be raised to the fullness of their humanity. People who learn without being taught are more like animals than men. And the school system must be so organized that all, old and young, rich and poor, noble and low, men and women, be taught effectively, not just symbolically and ostentatiously.

These are the thoughts written by the potential president of Harvard. But he never crossed the Atlantic. By the time Winthrop met him, he had already accepted the invitation of the Swedish government to organize a national system of schools for Queen Christina. Unlike Nebrija, he never had to argue the need for his services – they were always in great demand. The domain of the vernacular, considered untouchable by Isabella, had become the hunting ground for job-seeking Spanish *letrados*, Jesuits, and Czech divines. A sphere of formal education had been disembedded. Formally taught mother tongue professionally handled according to abstract rules had begun to compare with and encroach upon the vernacular. This gradual replacement and degradation of the vernacular by its costly counterfeit heralds the coming of the market-intensive society in which we now live.

Vernacular comes from an Indo-Germanic root that implies 'rootedness' and 'abode'. *Vernaculum* as a Latin word was used for whatever was homebred, homespun, homegrown, home-made, as opposed to what was obtained in formal exchange. The child of one's slave and of one's wife, the donkey born of one's own beast, were vernacular beings, as was the staple that came from the garden or the commons. If Karl Polanyi had adverted to this fact, he might have used the term in the meaning accepted by the ancient Romans: sustenance derived from reciprocity patterns imbedded in every aspect of life, as distinguished from sustenance that comes from exchange or from vertical distribution.

Vernacular was used in this general sense from preclassical times down to the technical formulations found in the Codex of Theodosius. It was Varro who picked the term to introduce the same distinction in language. For him, *vernacular speech* is made up of the words and patterns grown on the speaker's own ground, as opposed to what is grown elsewhere and then transported. And since Varro's authority was widely recognized, his definition stuck. He was the librarian of both Caesar and Augustus and the first Roman to attempt a thorough and critical study of the Latin language. His *Lingua Latina* was a basic reference book for centuries. Quintillian admired him as the most learned of all Romans. And Quintillian, the Spanish-born drill master for the future senators of Rome, is always proposed to normal students as one of the founders of their profession. But neither can be compared to Nebrija. Both Varro and Quintillian were concerned with shaping the speech of senators and scribes, the speech of the forum. Not so Nebrija; he sought control in the Queen's name over the everyday speech of all her people. Simply, Nebrija proposed to substitute a mother tongue for the vernacular.

Vernacular came into English in the one restricted sense to which Varro had confined its meaning. Just now, I would like to resuscitate some of its old breath. We need a simple, straightforward word to designate the activities of people when they are not motivated by thoughts of exchange, a word that denotes autonomous, non-market related actions through which people satisfy everyday needs – the actions that by their own true nature escape bureaucratic control, satisfying needs to which, in the very process, they give specific shape. Vernacular seems a good old word for this purpose, and should be acceptable to many contemporaries. There are technical words that designate the satisfaction of needs that economists do not or cannot measure – social production as opposed to economic production, the generation of use-values as opposed to the production of commodities, household economics as opposed to market economics. But these terms are specialized, tainted with some ideological prejudice, and each, in a different way, badly limps. Each contrasting pair of terms, in its own way, also fosters the confusion that assigns vernacular undertakings to unpaid, standardized, formalized activities. It is this kind of confusion I wish to clarify. We need a simple adjective to name those acts of competence, lust, or concern that we want to defend from measurement or manipulation by Chicago Boys and Socialist Commissars. The term must be broad enough to fit the preparation of food and the shaping of language, childbirth and recreation, without implying either a privatized activity akin to the housework of modern women, a hobby or an irrational and primitive procedure. Such an adjective is not at hand. But 'vernacular' might serve. By speaking about vernacular language and the possibility of its recuperation, I am trying to bring into awareness and discussion the existence of a vernacular mode of being, doing, and making that in a desirable future society might again expand in all aspects of life.

Mother tongue, since the term was first used, has never meant the vernacular, but rather its contrary. The term was first used by Catholic monks to designate a particular language they used, instead of Latin, when speaking from the pulpit. No Indo-Germanic culture before had used the term. The word was introduced into Sanskrit in the eighteenth century as a translation from the English. The term has no roots in the other major language families now spoken on which I could check. The only classical people who viewed their homeland as a kind of mother were the Cretans. Bachofen suggests that memories of an old matriarchal order still lingered in their culture. But even in Crete, there was no equivalent to 'mother' tongue. To trace the association which led to the term *mother tongue*, I shall first have to look at what happened at the court of Charlemagne, and then what happened later in the Abbey of Gorz.

The idea that humans are born in such fashion that they need institutional service from professional agents in order to reach that humanity for which by birth all people are destined can be traced down to Carolingian times. It was then that, for the first time in history, it was discovered that there are certain basic needs, needs that are universal to mankind and that cry out for satisfaction in a standard fashion that cannot be met in a vernacular way. The discovery is perhaps best associated with the Church reform that took place in the eighth century. The Scottish monk Alcuin, the former chancellor of York University who became the court philosopher of Charles the Great, played a prominent role in this reform. Up to that time the Church had considered its ministers primarily as priests, that is, as men selected and invested with special powers to meet communitary, liturgical, public needs. They were engaged in preaching at ritual occasions and had to preside at functions. They acted as public officials, analogous to those others through whom the state provided for the administration of justice, or, in Roman times, for public work. To think of these kinds of magistrates as if they were 'service professionals' would be an anachronistic projection of our contemporary categories.

But then, from the eighth century on, the classical priest rooted in Roman and Hellenistic models began to be transmogrified into the precursor of the service professional: the teacher, social worker, or educator. Church ministers began to cater to the personal needs of parishioners and to equip themselves with a sacramental and pastoral theology that defined and established these needs for their regular service. The institutionally defined care of the individual, the family, the village community, acquires unprecedented prominence. The term 'holy mother the church' ceases almost totally to mean the actual assembly of the faithful whose love, under the impulse of the Holy Spirit, engenders new life in the very act of meeting. The term *mother* henceforth refers to an invisible, mystical reality from which alone those services absolutely necessary for salvation can be obtained. Henceforth, access to the good graces of this mother on whom universally necessary salvation depends is entirely controlled by a hierarchy of ordained males. This gender-specific mythology of male hierarchies mediating access to the institutional source of life is without precedent. From the ninth to the eleventh century, the idea took shape that there are some needs common to all human beings that can be satisfied only through service from professional agents. Thus the definition of needs in terms of professionally defined commodities in the service sector precedes by a millennium the industrial production of universally needed basic goods.

Thirty-five years ago, Lewis Mumford tried to make this point. When I first read his statement that the monastic reform of the ninth century created some of the basic assumptions on which the industrial system is founded, I could not be convinced by something I considered more of an intuition than a proof. In the meantime, though, I have found a host of converging arguments – most of which Mumford does not seem to suspect – for rooting the ideologies of the industrial age in the earlier Carolingian Renaissance. The idea that there is no salvation without *personal services* provided by professionals in the name of an institutional Mother Church is one of these formerly unnoticed developments without which, again, our own age would be unthinkable. True, it took five hundred years of medieval theology to elaborate on this concept. Only by the end of the Middle Ages would the *pastoral* self-image of the Church be fully rounded. And only in the Council of Trent (1545) would this self-image of the Church as a mother milked by clerical hierarchies become formally defined. Then, in the *Constitution* of the Second Vatican Council (1964), the Catholic Church, which had served in the past as the prime model for the evolution of secular service organizations, aligns itself explicitly in the image of its secular imitations.

The important point here is the notion that the clergy can define its services as needs of human nature, and make this service-commodity the kind of necessity that cannot be forgone without jeopardy to eternal life. It is in this ability of a nonhereditary élite that we ought to locate the foundation without which the contemporary service or welfare state would not be conceivable. Surprisingly little research has been done on the religious concepts that fundamentally distinguish the industrial age from all other epochs. The official decline of the vernacular conception of Christian life in favor of one organized around pastoral care is a complex and drawn-out process constituting the background for a set of consistent shifts in the language and institutional development of the West.

When Europe first began to take shape as an idea and as a political reality, between Merovingian times and the High Middle Ages, what people spoke was unproblematic. It was called 'romance' or 'theodisc' – peoplish. Only somewhat later, *lingua vulgaris* became the common denominator distinguishing popular speech from the Latin of administration and doctrine. Since Roman times, a person's first language was the *patrius sermo*, the language of the male head of the household. Each such *sermo* or speech was perceived as a separate language. Neither in ancient Greece nor in the Middle Ages did people make the modern distinction between mutually understandable dialects and different languages. The same holds true today, for example, at the grass roots in India. What we know today as monolingual communities were and, in fact, are exceptions. From the Balkans to Indochina's western frontiers, it is still rare to find a village in which one cannot get along in more than two or three tongues. While it is assumed that each person has his *patrius sermo*, it is equally taken for granted that most persons speak several 'vulgar' tongues, each in a vernacular, untaught way. Thus the vernacular, in opposition to specialized, learned language – Latin for the Church, Frankish for the Court – was as obvious in its variety as the taste of local wines and food, as the shapes of house and hoe, down to the eleventh century. It is at this moment, quite suddenly, that the term *mother tongue* appears. It shows up in the sermons of some monks from the Abbey of Gorz. The process by which this phenomenon turns vernacular speech into a moral issue can only be touched upon here.

Gorz was a mother abbey in Lorraine, not far from Verdun. Benedictine monks had founded the monastery in the eighth century, around bones believed to belong to Saint Gorgonius. During the ninth century, a time of widespread decay in ecclesiastical discipline, Gorz, too, suffered a notorious decline. But only three generations after such scandalous dissolution Gorz became the center of monastic reform in the Germanic areas of the Empire. Its reinvigoration of Cistercian life paralleled the work of the reform abbey of Cluny. Within a century, 160 daughter abbeys throughout the northeastern parts of central Europe were established from Gorz.

It seems quite probable that Gorz was then at the center of the diffusion of a new technology that was crucial for the later imperial expansion of the European powers: the transformation of the horse into the tractor of choice. Four Asiastic inventions – the horseshoe, the fixed saddle and stirrup, the bit, and the cummett (the collar resting on the shoulder) – permitted important and extensive changes. One horse could replace six oxen. While supplying the same traction, and more speed, a horse could be fed on the acreage needed for one yoke of oxen. Because of its speed, the horse permitted a more extensive cultivation of the wet, northern soils, in spite of the short summers. Also, greater rotation of crops was possible. But even more importantly, the peasant could now tend fields twice as far away from his dwelling. A new pattern of life became possible. Formerly, people had lived in clusters of homesteads; now they could form villages large enough to support a parish and, later, a school. Through dozens of abbeys, monastic learning and discipline, together with the reorganization of settlement patterns, spread throughout this part of Europe.

Gorz lies close to the line that divides Frankish from Romance types of vernacular, and some monks from Cluny began to cross this line. In these circumstances, the monks of Gorz made language, vernacular language, into an issue to defend their territorial claims. The monks began to preach in Frankish, and spoke specifically about the value of the Frankish tongue. They began to use the pulpit as a forum to stress the importance of language itself, perhaps even to teach it. From the little we know, they used at least two approaches. First, Frankish was the language spoken by the women, even in those areas where the men were already beginning to use a Romance vernacular. Second, it was the language now used by Mother Church.

How charged with sacred meanings motherhood was in the religiosity of the twelfth century one can grasp through contemplating the contemporary statues of the Virgin Mary, or from reading the liturgical Sequences, the poetry of the time. The term mother tongue, from its very first use, instrumentalizes everyday language in the service of an institutional cause. The word was translated from Frankish into Latin. Then, as a rare Latin term, it incubated for several centuries. In the decades before Luther, quite suddenly and dramatically, mother tongue acquired a strong meaning. It came to mean the language created by Luther in order to translate the Hebrew Bible, the language taught by schoolmasters to read that book, and then the language that justified the existence of nation states.

Today, 'mother tongue' means several things: the first language learned by the child, and the language which the authorities of the state have decided ought to be one's first language. Thus, mother tongue can mean the first language picked up at random, generally a very different speech from the one taught by paid educators and by parents who act as if they were such educators. We see, then, that people are considered as creatures who need to be taught to speak properly in order 'to communicate' in the modern world – as they need to be wheeled about in motorized carriages in order to move in modern landscapes, their feet no longer fit. Dependence on taught mother tongue can be taken as the paradigm of all other dependencies typical of humans in an age of commodity-defined needs. And the ideology of this dependence was formulated by Nebrija. The ideology which claims that human mobility depends not on feet and open frontiers, but on the availability of 'transportation' is only slightly more than a hundred years old. Language teaching created employment long ago; macadam and the suspended coach made the conveyance of people a big business only from about the middle of the eighteenth century.

As language teaching has become a job, it has begun to cost a lot of money. Words are now one of the two largest categories of marketed values that make up the gross national product (GNP). Money decides what shall be said, who shall say it, when and what kind of people shall be targeted for the messages. The higher the cost of each uttered word, the more determined the echo demanded. In schools people learn to speak as they should. Money is spent to make the poor speak more like the wealthy, the sick more like the healthy; and the minority more like the majority. We pay to improve, correct, enrich, update the language of children and of their teachers. We spend more on the professional jargons that are taught in college, and more yet in high schools, to give teenagers a smattering of these jargons; but just enough to make them feel dependent on the psychologist, druggist, or librarian who is fluent in some special kind of English. We go even further: we first allow standard language to degrade ethnic, black, or hillbilly language, and then spend money to teach their counterfeits as academic subjects. Administrators and entertainers, admen and newsmen, ethnic politicians and 'radical' professionals, form powerful interest groups, each fighting for a larger slice of the language pie.

I do not really know how much is spent in the United States to make words. But soon someone will provide us with the necessary statistical tables. Ten years ago, energy accounting was almost unthinkable. Now it has become an established practice. Today you can easily look up how many 'energy units' have gone into growing, harvesting, packaging, transporting, and merchandising one edible calory of bread. The difference between the bread produced and eaten in a village in Greece and that found in an American supermarket is enormous – about forty times more energy units are contained in each edible calory of the latter. Bicycle traffic in cities permits one to move four times as fast as on foot for one-fourth of the energy expended – while cars, for the same progress, need 150 times as many calories per passenger mile. Information of this kind was available ten years ago, but no one thought about it. Today, it is recorded and will soon lead to a change in people's outlook on the need for fuels. It would now be interesting to know what language accounting looks like, since the linguistic analysis of contemporary language is certainly not complete, unless for each group of speakers we know the amount of money spent on shaping the speech of the average person. Just as social energy accounts are only approximate and at best allow us to identify the orders of magnitude within which the relative values are found, so language accounting would provide us with data on the relative prevalence of standardized, taught language in a population – sufficient, however, for the argument I want to make.

But mere per capita expenditure employed to mold the language of a group of speakers does not tell us enough. No doubt we would learn that each paid word addressed to the rich costs, per capita, much more than words addressed to the poor.

Watts are actually more democratic than words. But taught language comes in a vast range of qualities. The poor, for instance, are much more blared at than the rich, who can buy tutoring and, what is more precious, hedge on their own high class vernacular by purchasing silence. The educator, politician and entertainer now come with a loudspeaker to Oaxaca, to Travancore, to the Chinese commune, and the poor immediately forfeit the claim to that indispensable luxury, the silence out of which vernacular language arises.

Yet even without putting a price-tag on silence, even without the more detailed language economics on which I would like to draw, I can still estimate that the dollars spent to power any nation's motors pale before those that are now expended on prostituting speech in the mouths of paid speakers. In rich nations, language has become incredibly spongy, absorbing huge investments. Generous expenditure to cultivate the language of the mandarin, the author, the actor, or the charmer have always been a mark of high civilization. But these were efforts to teach élites special codes. Even the cost of making some people learn secret languages in traditional societies is incomparably lower than the capitalization of language in industrial societies.

In poor countries today, people still speak to each other without the experience of capitalized language, although such countries always contain a tiny élite who manage very well to allocate a larger proportion of the national income for their prestige language. Let me ask: What is different in the everyday speech of groups whose language has received – or shall I say absorbed? resisted? survived? suffered? enjoyed? – huge investments, and the speech of people whose language has remained outside the market? Comparing these two worlds of language, I want to focus my curiosity on just one issue that arises in this context. Does the structure and function of the language itself change with the rate of investment? Are these alterations such that all languages that absorb funds show changes in the same direction? In this introductory exploration of the subject, I cannot demonstrate that this is the case. But I do believe my arguments make both propositions highly probable, and show that structurally oriented language economics are worth exploring.

Taught everyday language is without precedent in pre-industrial cultures. The current dependence on paid teachers and models of ordinary speech is just as much a unique characteristic of industrial economies as dependence on fossil fuels. The need for taught mother tongue was discovered four centuries earlier, but only in our generation have both language and energy been effectively treated as worldwide needs to be satisfied for all people by planned, programmed production and distribution. Because, unlike the vernacular of capitalized language, we can reasonably say that it results from *production*.

Traditional cultures subsisted on sunshine, which was captured mostly through agriculture. The hoe, the ditch, the yoke, were basic means to harness the sun. Large sails or waterwheels were known, but rare. These cultures that lived mostly on the sun subsisted basically on vernacular values. In such societies, tools were essentially the prolongation of arms, fingers, and legs. There was no need for the production of power in centralized plants and its distant distribution to clients. Equally, in these essentially sun-powered cultures, there was no need for language production. Language was drawn by each one from the cultural environment, learned from the encounter with people whom the learner could smell and touch, love or hate. The vernacular spread just as most things and services were shared, namely, by multiple forms of mutual reciprocity, rather than clientage to the appointed teacher or professional. Just as fuel was not delivered, so the vernacular was never taught. Taught tongues did exist, but they were rare, as rare as sails and sills. In most cultures, we know that speech resulted from conversation embedded in everyday life, from listening to fights and lullabies, gossip, stories, and dreams. Even today, the majority of people in poor countries learn all their language skills without any paid tutorship, without any attempt whatsoever to teach them how to speak. And they learn to speak in a way that nowhere compares with the self-conscious, self-important, colorless mumbling that, after a long stay in villages in South America and Southeast Asia, always shocks me when I visit an American college. I feel sorrow for those students whom education has made tone deaf; they have lost the faculty for hearing the difference between the dessicated utterance of standard television English and the living speech of the un-schooled. What else can I expect, though, from people who are not brought up at a mother's breast, but on formula? On canned milk, if they are from poor families, and on a brew prepared under the nose of Ralph Nader if they are born among the enlightened? For people trained to choose between packaged formulas, mother's breast appears as just one more option. And in the same way, for people who were intentionally *taught* to listen and to speak, untutored vernacular seems just like another, albeit less developed, model among many.

But this is simply false. Language exempt from rational tutor-ship is a different kind of social phenomenon from language that is purposefully taught. Where untutored language is the predominant marker of a shared world, a sense of power within the group exists, and this sense cannot be duplicated by lan-guage that is delivered. One way this difference shows is the sense of power over language itself, over its acquisition. Even today, the poor in non-industrial countries all over the world are polyglot. My friend, the goldsmith in Timbuktu, speaks Songhay at home, listens to Bambara on the radio, devotedly and with some understanding says his prayers five times a day in Arabic, gets along in two trade languages on the Souk, con-verses in passable French that he picked up in the army – and none of these languages was formally taught him. He did not set out to learn these tongues; each is one style in which he remembers a peculiar set of experiences that fits into the frame of that language. Communities in which monolingual people prevail are rare except in three kinds of settings: tribal com-munities that have not really experienced the late neolithic, communities that for a long time lived through exceptional forms of discrimination, and among the citizens of nation states that, for several generations, have enjoyed the benefits of com-pulsory schooling. To take it for granted that most people are monolingual is typical of the members of the middle class. Admiration for the vernacular polyglot unfailingly exposes the social climber.

Throughout history, untutored language was prevalent, but it was hardly ever the only kind of language known. Just as in traditional cultures some energy was captured through wind-mills and canals, and those who had large boats or those who cornered the right spot on the brook could use their tool for a net transfer of power to their own advantage, so some people have always used a taught language to corner some privilege. But such additional codes remained either rare and special, or served very narrow purposes. The ordinary language, until Nebrija, was prevalently vernacular. And this vernacular, be it the ordinary colloquial, a trade idiom, the language of prayer, the craft jargon, the language of basic accounts, the language of venery or of age (for example, baby talk) was learned on the side, as part of meaningful everyday life. Of course, Latin or Sanskrit were formally taught to the priest, court languages such as Frankish or Persian or Turkish were taught to the future scribe. Neophytes were formally initiated into the language of astronomy, alchemy, or late masonry. And, clearly, the knowledge of such formally taught languages raised a man above others, somewhat like the saddle lifts the free man above the serfs in the infantry, or the bridge lifts the captain above the crew. But even when access to some élite language was unlocked by a formal initiation, it did not necessarily mean that language was being taught. Quite frequently, the process of formal initiation did not transfer to the initiate a new language skill, but simply exempted him henceforth from a taboo that forbade others to use certain words, or to speak out on certain occasions. Male initiation in the language of the hunt or of sex is probably the most widespread example of such a ritually selective language de-tabooization.

But, in traditional societies, no matter how much or how little language was taught, the taught language rarely rubbed off on vernacular speech. Neither the existence of some language teaching at all times nor the spread of some language through professional preachers or comedians weakens my main point: outside of those societies that we now call Modern European, no attempt was made to impose on entire populations an everyday language that would be subject to the control of paid teachers or announcers. Everyday language, until recently, was nowhere the product of design; it was nowhere paid for and delivered like a commodity. And while every historian who deals with the origins of nation states pays attention to the imposition of a national tongue, economists generally overlook the fact that this taught mother tongue is the earliest of specifically modern commodities, the model of all 'basic needs' to come.

Before I can go on to contrast taught colloquial speech and vernacular speech, costly language and that which comes at no cost, I must clarify one more distinction. Between taught mother tongue and the vernacular I draw the line of demarcation somewhere else than linguists when they distinguish the high language of an élite from the dialect spoken in lower classes, somewhere other than the frontier that separates regional and superregional languages, somewhere else than restricted and corrected code, and somewhere else than at the line between the language of the literate and the illiterate. No matter how restricted within geographic boundaries, no matter how distinctive for a social level, no matter how specialized for one sex role or one caste, language can be either vernacular (in the sense in which I here use the term) or of the taught variety. Elite language, trade language, second language, local idiom, are nothing new. But each of these can be formally taught and the taught counterfeit of the vernacular comes as a commodity and is something entirely new.

The contrast between these two complementary forms is most marked and important in taught everyday language, that is, taught colloquial, taught standardized everyday speech. But here again we must avoid confusion. Not all standard language is either grammar-ridden or taught. In all of history, one mutually understandable dialect has tended toward predominance in a given region. This kind of principal dialect was often accepted as the standard form. It was indeed written more frequently than other dialects, but not, for that reason, was it taught. Rather, diffusion occurred through a much more complex and subtle process. Midland English, for example, slowly emerged as that second, common style in which people born into any English dialect could also speak their own tongue. Quite suddenly, the language of Mogul hordes (Urdu) came into being in northern India. Within two generations, it became the standard in Hindustan, the trade language in a vast area, and the medium for exquisite poetry written in the Arabic and Sanskrit alphabets. Not only was this language not taught for several generations, but poets who wanted to perfect their

competence explicitly avoided the study of Hindu-Urdu; they
explored the Persian, Arabic, or Sanskrit sources that had
originally contributed to its being. In Indonesia, in half a
generation of resistance to Japanese and Dutch, the militant
fraternal and combative slogans, posters, and secret radios of
the freedom struggle spread Malay competence into every
village, and did so much more effectively than the later efforts
of the Ministry of Language Control that was established after
independence.

It is true that the dominant position of élite or standard
language was always bolstered by the technique of writing.
Printing enormously enhanced the colonizing power of élite
language. But to say that because printing was invented élite
language is destined to supplant vernacular variety results from
a debilitated imagination – like saying that after the atom bomb
only super powers shall be sovereign. The historical monopoly
of educational bureaucracies over the printing press is no argument that printing techniques cannot be used to give new
vitality to written expression and new literary opportunity to
thousands of vernacular forms. The fact that the printing press
could augment the extent and power of ungovernable vernacular readings was the source of Nebrija's greatest concern and of
his argument *against* the vernacular. The fact that printing was
used since the early sixteenth century (but not during the first
forty years of its existence) primarily for the imposition of
standard colloquials does not mean that printed language must
always be a taught form. The commercial status of taught
mother tongue, call it national language, literary standard, or
television language, rests largely on unexamined axioms, some
of which I have already mentioned: that printing implies
standardized composition; that books written in the standard
language could not be easily read by people who had not been
schooled in that tongue; that reading is by its very nature a
silent activity that usually should be conducted in private; that
enforcing a universal ability to read a few sentences and then
copy them in writing increases the access of a population to the
content of libraries: these and other such illusions are used to
enhance the standing of teachers, the sale of rotary presses, the
grading of people according to their language code and, up to
now, an increase in the GNP.

Vernacular spreads by practical use; it is learned from people who mean what they say and who say what they mean to the person they address in the context of everyday life. This is not so in taught language. With taught language, the one from whom I learn is not a person whom I care for or dislike, but a professional speaker. The model for taught colloquial is somebody who does not say what he means, but who recites what others have contrived. In this sense, a street vendor announcing his wares in ritual language is not a professional speaker, while the King's herald or the clown on television are the prototypes. Taught colloquial is the language of the announcer who follows the script that an editor was told by a publicist that a board of directors had decided should be said. Taught colloquial is the dead, impersonal rhetoric of people paid to declaim with phony conviction texts composed by others, who themselves are usually paid only for *designing* the text. People who speak taught language imitate the announcer of news, the comedian of gag writers, the instructor following the teacher's manual to explain the textbook, the songster of engineered rhymes, or the ghost-written president. This is language that implicitly lies when I use it to say something to your face; it is meant for the spectator who watches the scene. It is the language of farce, not of theater, the language of the hack, not of the true performer. The language of the media always seeks the appropriate audience profile that the sponsor tries to hit and to hit hard. While the vernacular is engendered in me by the intercourse between complete persons locked in conversation with each other, taught language is syntonic with loudspeakers whose assigned job is gab.

The vernacular and taught mother tongue are like the two extremes on the spectrum of the colloquial. Language would be totally inhuman if it were totally taught. That is what Humboldt meant when he said that real language is speech that can only be fostered, never taught like mathematics. Speech is much more than communication, and only machines can communicate without reference to vernacular roots. Their chatter with one another in New York now takes up about three-quarters of the lines that the telephone company operates under a franchise that guarantees access by people. This is an obvious perversion of a legal privilege that results from political aggrandizement and the degradation of vernacular domains to second-class commodities. But even more embarrassing and depressing than this abuse of a forum of free speech by robots is the incidence of robot-like stock phrases that blight the remaining lines on which people presumably 'speak' to each other. A growing percentage of speech has become mere formula in content and style. In this way, the colloquial moves on the spectrum of language increasingly from vernacular to capital-intensive 'communication', as if it were nothing more than the human variety of the exchange that also goes on between bees, whales, and computers. True, some vernacular elements or aspects always survive – but that is the case even for most computer programs. I do not claim that the vernacular dies; only that it withers. The American, French, or German colloquials have become composites made up of two kinds of language: commodity-like taught uniquack and a limping, ragged, jerky vernacular struggling to survive. Taught mother tongue has established a radical monopoly over speech, just as transportation has over mobility or, more generally, commodity over vernacular values.

A resistance, sometimes as strong as a sacred taboo, prevents people shaped by life in industrial society from recognizing the difference with which we are dealing – the difference between capitalized language and the vernacular, which comes at no economically measurable cost. It is the same kind of inhibition that makes it difficult for those who are brought up within the industrial system to sense the fundamental distinction between nurture from the breast and feeding by bottle, between literature and textbook, between a mile moved on my own and a passenger mile – areas where I have discussed this issue over the past years.

Most people would probably be willing to admit that there is a huge difference in taste, meaning, and satisfaction between a home-cooked meal and a TV dinner. But the examination and understanding of this difference can be easily blocked, especially among those committed to equal rights, equity and service to the poor. They know how many mothers have no milk in their breasts, how many children in the South Bronx suffer protein deficiencies, how many Mexicans – surrounded by fruit trees – are crippled by vitamin deficits. As soon as I raise the distinction between vernacular values and values susceptible of economic measurement and, therefore, of being administered, some self-appointed tutor of the so-called proletariat will tell me that I am avoiding the critical issue by giving importance to non-economic niceties. Should we not seek first the just distribution of commodities that correlate to basic needs? Poetry and fishing shall then be added without more thought or effort. So goes the reading of Marx and the Gospel of St. Matthew as interpreted by the theology of liberation.

A laudable intention here attempts an argument that should have been recognized as illogical in the nineteenth century, and that countless experiences have shown false in the twentieth. So far, every single attempt to substitute a universal commodity for a vernacular value has led, not to equality, but to a hierarchical modernization of poverty. In the new dispensation, the poor are no longer those who survive by their vernacular activities because they have only marginal or no access to the market. No, the modernized poor are those whose vernacular domain, in speech and in action, is most restricted – those who get least satisfaction out of the few vernacular activities in which they can still engage.

The second-level taboo which I have set out to violate is not constituted by the distinction between the vernacular and taught mother tongue, nor by the destruction of the vernacular through the radical monopoly of taught mother tongue over speech, nor even by the class-biased intensity of this vernacular paralysis. Although these three matters are far from being clearly understood today, they have been widely discussed in the recent past. The point at issue which is sedulously overlooked is quite another: Mother tongue is taught increasingly, not by paid agents, but by unpaid parents. These latter deprive their own children of the last opportunity to listen to adults who have something to say to each other. This was brought home to me clearly, some time ago, while back in New York City in an area that a few decades earlier I had known quite well, the South Bronx. I went there at the request of a young college teacher, married to a colleague. This man wanted my signature on a petition for compensatory pre-kindergarten language training for the inhabitants of a partially burnt-out, high-rise slum. Twice already, quite decidedly and yet with deep embarrassment, I had refused. To overcome my resistance against this expansion of educational services, he took me on visits to brown, white, black, mostly single-parent so-called households. I saw dozens of children dashing through uninhabitable cement corridors, exposed all day to blaring television and radio in English, Spanish and even Yiddish. They seemed equally lost in language and landscape. As my friend pressed for my signature, I tried to argue for the protection of these children against further castration and inclusion in the educational sphere. We talked at cross-purposes, unable to meet. And then, in the evening, at dinner in my friend's home, I suddenly understood why. This man, whom I viewed with awe because he had chosen to live in this hell, had ceased to be a parent and had become a total teacher. In front of their own children this couple stood *in loco magistri*. Their children had to grow up without parents, because these two adults, in every word they addressed to their two sons and one daughter, were 'educating' them – they were at dinner constantly conscious that they were modeling the speech of their children, and they asked me to do the same.

For the professional parent who engenders children as a professional lover, who volunteers his semi-professional counseling skills for neighborhood organizations, the distinction between his unpaid contribution to the managed society and what could be, in contrast, the recovery of vernacular domains, remains meaningless. He is fit prey for a new type of growth-oriented ideology – the planning and organization of an expanding shadow economy, the last frontier of arrogance which *homo economicus* faces.

IV
RESEARCH BY PEOPLE

THE term, 'science *by* people', came up in the seventies and is now quite common. It appears mostly in the kind of literature for which the Borremans bibliography is the best guide,* among the multifaceted, decentralized community of authors who unplug themselves from consumption and use modern procedures to live simple, uncluttered and more autonomous lives. I have been asked to clarify my understanding of the term which they use to designate their research activities. It is a new term which, at first, seems slippery and ideological. One finds no antecedents for it in the recent past. I have the impression that those who use it intend a meaning which is the exact inverse of what science has signified ever since Bacon, or even since the thirteenth century.

My survey of the Borremans literature shows that 'science *by* people' is used in opposition to 'science *for* people'. The latter designates something called Research and Development or, since World War II, simply 'R & D'. R & D is usually conducted by large institutions – governments, industry, universities, clinics, the military, foundations. It is also carried out by small teams of enterprising persons who hope to sell their research results to institutions. It is a highly prestigious activity, done for the common good – so its supporters and practitioners claim – expensive and tax-exempt. It provides regular well-paid jobs for academics with advanced degrees. R & D can be social or natural, fundamental or applied, specialized or interdisciplinary. The use of the term 'science *for* people', as applied to R & D does not usually imply reproach; in principle, it does not signify disapproval of an endeavor. It simply means that the

* Valentina Borremans, Guide to Convivial Tools. Library Journal Special Report 13. Published by RR Bowker, 1180 6th Ave, NY 10036, 1979

results of the research have no bearing on the immediate every-day activities of him or her who does it. R & D can be carried out on neutron bombs, muscular distrophy, solar cells or fish ponds – always for the service of *other* people. Obviously, 'science *by* people' is not this.

Initially, the use of the term 'science *by* people' might be interpreted as sour grapes. It designates research that is done with few or no funds, no sponsorship, no access to publication in the prestigious journals, producing results that are without interest to the supermarket. Yet the people who do it seem neither jilted nor on the make. They do careful, methodical and disciplined research, are fully informed of the R & D in related areas, use these results when applicable, and in only one decade have built up an alternative network of publications which provides a forum for the diffusion and criticism of their efforts. They work alone or in tiny teams, primarily for results that directly shape their mode and style of living, are uninterested in patents and rarely produce finished products for sale. They give no impression of being the poor cousins of those working in R & D.

Intuitively, it is easy to recognize the distinction between this research and R & D. In the former, people concentrate on con-structing, improving or beautifying the tools and immediate environment which serve them directly, leaving to others the task of imitating or adapting what they do. In practical use, the distinction is clear. But most discussion of this distinction so far has been hazy, emotional, ideological or beside the point. When best formulated the distinction so far has remained a negative one. A good example is that of Borremans herself: "Science by people is . . . research done to increase the use-value of daily activities without increasing the person's dependence on the market or professions."

'Research by people' does convey a search for something which is widely practiced yet difficult to name in twentieth cen-tury language. The activity clearly is research, not an assort-ment of hit or miss tryouts. It is supported by library surveys and critically evaluated by peers around the globe. It represents an effort to unplug its practitioner from the market. It is a search for autonomy, but in a new synthesis, not in a return to the 'good old days' or in an imitation of Amish community living. Such research is not a hobby, nor a religious enterprise. And since it primarily seeks to improve the actual comfort or beauty of those who do it and critically tests the results, research by people cannot be called utopian in any accepted sense. A set of intensions and activities which fits these criteria is something patently new. No one word can express it. Faute de mieux, let us stick to the term '. . . *by* people'.

As a historian, I am very suspicious of anything which pretends to be totally new. If I cannot find precedents for an idea, I immediately suspect that it is a foolish one. If I cannot find anyone in the past with whom I am acquainted, and in my fancy can discuss with him what surprises me, I feel very lonely, a prisoner of my own present-day and parochial horizon. Therefore, when I was challenged to clarify the meaning of research by people I looked around and finally found Hugh of St. Victor, a twelfth century thinker who has proved to be excellent company. Living before the thirteenth century, but after classical antiquity, he is untainted by what we conventionally call science.

Hugh of St. Victor was born around 1096, probably in the Flemish town of Ypres, and grew up in Saxony. To his own century, he was known as Hugh of St. Victor (where he taught), Magister Hugo, Venerabilis Hugo, Hugh the Great. He was also called Hugh the Saxon, because he spent his youth in the Monastery of Hamersleben and later some imputed noble birth to him from the reigning house of Blankenburg. He deserves an important place in the philosophy of technology, since he dealt with the subject in an original way, quite distinct from any other author I know. But up to now his ideas have never been examined for the potential contribution they could make to the current attempt to identify the alternative to R & D. Mindful of this, I find it quite significant that he is not discussed in the major histories of science and technology. At best, one sometimes finds him in a cursory list along with ten other names. Therefore, before I can discuss his ideas, I must first make him come alive.

As a young man, he joined a new kind of religious order the Canons Regular. These were not monks, but communities of men brought into existence by the recent demographic changes in Europe, principally the rise of the free city. The rule and practice of monks prescribed a life in small rural communities, often quite isolated. They tended to live in self-sufficient enclaves, surrounded by newly cleared land. Their activities were confined almost exclusively to the liturgy and physical labor in the management of their monasteries and fields. The new canons, on the other hand, usually established themselves in the cities, committed to a life of exemplary virtue for the edification of the Christian population.

As a young man, with his uncle, Hugh traveled from Saxony to Paris, where he settled in the Augustinian cloister of St. Victor, then still outside the city walls. Paris teemed with intellectual excitement. Men of immense learning, filled with deep passion for their convictions, acting and speaking out with shameless simplicity, clashed in public controversy. The center of all this spiritual ferment was still the Cathedral school, from which the university would evolve seventy years later. Peter Abelard was prefect. A brilliant cleric with a biting and incisive wit, one of the great teachers of the West, he was idolized by his students. But more than one of Abelard's colleagues, the teachers at the school, were driven into exile by his ridicule. Hugh's own master, William of Champeaux, was among them. Abelard's teaching was decisive in renewing critical procedures and methods in thought. In the midst of an age dominated by faith and obedience, he insisted on the value of methodical doubt. He demonstrated the necessity of doubt by juxtaposing the contrary opinions of respected authorities against each other, and by emphasizing the role of reason when such conflicts between traditions and authors had to be resolved. In ethics, he applied analogous principles, stressing conscience and intention in an age of ritual and legalism. He had powerful enemies. The great mystic, Bernard of Clairvaux, noble and austere, the violent reformer of Benedictine monasticism and preacher of the crusade, was the driving spirit infusing a lifelong witchhunt to silence Abelard. For Bernard, philosophy and the humanities fitted a monk's and scholar's life only to the degree necessary for a better grasp of Holy Writ.

Abelard's enemies achieved a temporary triumph. Because of his notorious affair with Héloïse, the most brilliant of his pupils, he was chased from his chair, gelded and dishonored. Probably at this moment, Hugh arrived in Paris to teach about the place of science in human life. We find the first documentary evidence for Hugh's presence in this milieu when he was already the recognized Master of St. Victor in a double sense – he was the director of studies, and exercised the powerful intellectual influence which would extend beyond his own lifetime. For two generations, St. Victor owed its odd mixture of down-to-earth mysticism, both tender and humorously critical, to Hugh.

We know very little about his life. Few anecdotes are told about him. He probably traveled to Rome once. But those who read his works have no difficulty in identifying the original and unique character of his ideas. They are all marked by a strong personal style. His repeated advice to his students seems to have been: learn everything; with time, you will find out that none of it was acquired in vain. E. R. Curtius knows of no earlier theologian who would have recommended laughter to Christians. Hugh even encouraged teachers to foster merriment among their students, since serious matters are absorbed more easily and with more pleasure when they are mixed with humor. Such a recommendation flew straight in the face of at least 700 years of Christian exhortation to students to shun not only the flesh but also the laughter which ripples it. Until his last moment, Hugh maintained his high spirits, as Osberg, the Brother who nursed him to the end, records. This monastic doorman relates that throngs of people came to visit his tomb, but ugly rumors also began to circulate in Paris: students, probably from among the Cistercian monks, then very distrustful of technical progress, complained that Hugh's ghost visited them at night. He came to ask for prayers, needed to release him from purgatory where he was doing penance for his exaggerated curiosity about scientific and mechanical matters.

Hugh's posthumous influence was felt far beyond his own cloister where he had faithful but, on the whole, flat-footed disciples. He influenced the famous Dominicans, Albert the Great and his student, Thomas Aquinas, the Franciscan masters, Alexander of Hales and Bonaventure. His thought and statements years later became popular reading in the *Imitation of Christ*. He is among the few medieval thinkers quoted by Kierkegaard. But his clearest and broadest influence occurred through the use of his work, *Didascalicon*, which became a textbook.

The middle of the twelfth century constituted one of those rare moments in history when scholars possess a confident sense that the mastery of the works of the past is about to reach a natural end. The thought of Greece, Rome and the Church Fathers seemed assimilated. Thinkers began to feel comfortable about their command of the past's achievements. St. Bernard, Abelard and Hugh of St. Victor represented an entirely new kind of genius that flourished during the short period between 1110 and 1150 – thinkers who, having thoroughly digested their tradition, now felt free to create a new synthesis. The scientific and metaphysical works of Aristotle had not yet reached and upset Paris. They had not yet been translated from the Arabic, and their Arab commentators were still unknown. During this creative lull, some of the West's greatest textbooks were written: Peter the Lombard's *Sentences* (1150), Gratian's *Concordances of the Law* (1140), and the first of them, Hugh's *Didascalicon* (c. 1127). These books remained in use and became obligatory reading for those who sought a liberal education right into the seventeenth century – a part of every cleric's, indeed, every scholar's formation. As school books, with the exception of grammars, they had an extraordinary lifetime. The end of their undisputed acceptance marks the conclusion of the Middle Ages much more decisively than either the Renaissance or the Reformation.

In view of this lengthy and extensive renown, it is highly significant that his fiercely original thoughts on mechanical science went unobserved and unnoted. Hugh defined mechanical science as that part of philosophy which studies remedies for bodily weakness, when such weakness derives from humanly-caused disruptions in the environment – science, then, is a corrective for an ecological disorder. Asked to clarify the notion of a new conception of science which underlies the various 'movements' of science by people, I know of no better approach than a confrontation with Hugh of St. Victor's thought.

It would be beyond the scope of this essay to introduce the reader to Hugh's central concerns about metaphor, analogy, mystical knowledge and love. Therefore, I must tear out of their context his reflections on science as an aid, remedy or cure and the scientific aspect of the mechanical arts. But, to make his thought understood, I must explain a bit about his perception of the human condition. He accepted the story of man's origins, as related in Genesis. God first created Adam and, out of him, Eve. He made them so that they might live in harmony with the rest of creation. When he appointed them gardeners of Eden, he gave them an exacting task, but one which implied no toil.

Hugh strongly believed that God made each thing according to its own beauty. This insistence on beauty, and on the visual perception of reality, is characteristic of him. He gave three sets of 'eyes' to Adam and Eve – the eyes of the body, providing for ordinary cogitation; the eyes of reason, for meditating on the significance of eternal beauty for the beholder; and eyes fit for the contemplation of the Creator himself. This last set of eyes, made to look into blinding light, is designed to see the invisible, "what he is not, never what he is". The three sets of eyes are part of the basic endowment with which the Creator equipped human beings. For Hugh, the light which fired the three sets of eyes is the divine light, as reflected by nature: the soul and heaven in the mirror which is man.

Accepting the biblical story, he believed that certain restrictions had been imposed on the first couple by the Creator. They were free to use and enjoy the garden. But they were not to break the fruit from just one tree. In Hebrew, it is called the tree of *jadah* – meaning knowledge, penetration, power, possession. The serpent, however, a fallen angel, was envious of their exalted position within the universe. It persuaded Eve to break a branch and a fruit from just that one tree. Adam, Hugh insists, moved not by curiosity but by *affectus dilectionis* (a love of deep affection for Eve), ate what she offered him. As a consequence, the human world was upset. As the mirror of their eyes darkened, they felt ashamed. Simultaneously, nature, which they had offended and from which they had to obtain their sustenance, was accursed. Those who had been created to be the gardeners of Eden now had to be born from a bleeding womb and obtain their wherewithal from a field full of thistles. Created to be leisurely gardeners of Paradise, their own transgression of the rules of primordial nature compelled them henceforth to eke out their existence in sweat and frustration.

Hugh takes this historical understanding of ecology as the starting point of his general theory of science. Humans, through their own fault, are weakened and must survive in an environment they themselves have damaged. Science, then, is the search for a remedy for this painful condition. Thus the primary emphasis is the attempt to relieve human weakness, not to control, dominate or conquer nature for the purpose of turning it into a pseudo-paradise.

Hugh's metaphors fit the age of faith, not that of the quantum. He inhabits creation, not stellar space. History for him is that of salvation, not that of evolution. Yet, notwithstanding the distance between us, our approaches to ecology can be compared and contrasted. For Hugh ecology is the hypothesis from which the necessity of science derives; for R & D ecology is based on scientific assumptions. To grasp this, we must listen carefully to the language in which he writes.

Hugh was like a moving flame. Brought up in German, he lived in Paris, but his own language was Latin. This Latin was the kind of language which English speakers today experience great difficulty understanding. No one was born to it. Scholars learned its classical variety. But for scholars, scribes, religious and lawyers it then became the main language of everyday intercourse. Therefore, they felt entitled to shape it to their needs, their feelings, their whims. It was not a dead language, nor an élite language into which only some are born. It was the living language of a scholarly community, where all who used Latin acquired it relatively late in life. It is therefore a kind of tongue our age has lost. This fact makes any translation from medieval Latin a risky undertaking. For example, when Hugh speaks about *philosophia*, I strongly suspect that his meaning in contemporary English is much closer to 'science' than to 'philosophy'.

Hugh presents his general theory of philosophy (or, science) in two works: his textbook for a general introduction to advanced studies, the *Didascalicon*, and the *Dialogue of Dindimus on Philosophy*. The *Dialogue* was probably written a couple of years after the textbook. In it, Hugh hides behind the figure of a holy man from the pagan East, Dindimus, King of the Brahmans.

He took his figure out of a novel on Alexander the Great, which reached him in a Latin translation of Pseudo-Callisthenes. As interlocutors for Dindimus, he provides: Indaletus, the legendary apostle who converted southern Spain (at the time of Hugh, this region had been under Muslim domination for more than 400 years), and Sosthenes, the chief of the synagogue mentioned in the Acts of the Apostles (18.17). A subtle method lay in this apparently strange procedure. Hugh wanted to make a point which could not but offend many people. He wanted to give consistency to his ecological foundation of science without recourse to dogmas of faith. So he chose a virtuous pagan, a Brahmin, to make the argument for him. The Brahmin could insist, with more freedom than a Christian, that scientific inquiry was part of the human birthright, and could proceed unaided by Holy Writ. Hugh's choices were severely limited. Had he chosen a pre-Christian Greek, his readers could have argued that, after the coming of Christ, the situation of science had changed. Had he chosen a Muslim, his readers could have interpreted the latter as a hardened infidel arguing against the light of faith. So he chose an ascetic pagan, a man who, in the thought of the time, could be considered an unconscious Christian. To Dindimus he assigned the task of explaining the criterion that gives unity to philosophy/science, and the place of the mechanical arts within it.

When the first couple transgressed the order of nature, the disharmony thereby provoked clouded their eyesight. But it did not totally extinguish the eternal fire of truth, which continues to burn externally in the senses and, internally, in the imagination. This fire continuously kindles curiosity, surprise, admiration – the starting point of science. Science is the attempt to restore, however partially, that human competence which was lost in the original ecological catastrophe which started history on Earth. Science has three principal goals:

> . . . wisdom, virtue and competence to face needs. wisdom is the understanding of things as they are. Virtue is a habit of the heart, a habit which establishes harmony with reason in the way of nature. *Necessitas* [competence in the face of need] is something without which we cannot live, but without which

we would live more happily. These three things are as many remedies against the three evils to which human life is subject: wisdom against ignorance, virtue against vice, and competence against the body's weakness. In order to do away with the three evils, men have sought these remedies, and in order to reach them art and discipline were discovered. For wisdom, the theoretical arts were discovered; for virtue, the practical arts; for needs, the mechanical arts.

In this text, Hugh starts from *ignorantia*, the feebleness of the mind's eye, deprived of God's clear reflection. As a corrective, the mind needs theoretical science, a vision of things as they are. Such science leads to wisdom. Then Hugh deals with *vitium*, moral flabbiness, which requires the aid of *habitus animi*, stable habits of the soul – in the language of Erich Fromm we might translate as character. These one acquires in the ethical or social science, *practica*, which leads to virtue. Finally, we live out of harmony with nature. Because of our aggression, a kind of revenge imposes necessities on us. To live, we must face and overcome these necessities. This can be accomplished through recourse to what Hugh first calls mechanical science. *Theorica*, *practica* and *mechanica* are the three cures for personal weakness.

Dindimus argues that the element common to all science is the fact that it serves as a crutch for human weakness. As far as we know, Hugh was the first to reduce the invention of arts and science to certain defects in human nature. But we do not know whether this reduction is an invention of his own. It is certain, however, that the definition of science as a remedy for the weakness of the persons who engage in it, and who must engage in it in order to survive in an environment originally impaired by human action, is characteristic of Hugh alone. The idea is picked up by Richard of St. Victor (in his *Liber Exceptionum* – c. 1159), and last mentioned eighty years after Hugh's death. It is a view of science which is diametrically opposed to what began to take shape in the thirteenth century – when Aristotle was rediscovered – and to what is still dominant in the West. To see this opposition between Hugh's science and ours more clearly, perhaps we should stick to Hugh's term and, with Dindimus, speak about it as *philosophia* – as "the caring pursuit of truth, motivated not by that love which cherishes the well-known, but driven by the desire to pursue further what has been tasted and has been found pleasing", as Dindimus says. Now, this is definitely not what R & D is. Nor is it compatible with the Baconian attempt to subjugate nature. And, more importantly, it is not some pure, disinterested research which aims at finding and publishing the truth. This "caring pursuit of truth motivated . . . by what has been tasted and found pleasing", has no proper name today, unless 'science *by* people' be it. Those who thus label their own activities pursue something analogous to what Hugh meant by science, philosophy, the love of wisdom, when he defined it as the critical pursuit of remedies to self-induced weakness which will remain forever man's destiny in a world which has been marred by him.

For our reflection on 'science *by* people', Master Hugh has a second important contribution to make. He was original, not only with his ideas on science as a remedy, but also when he placed the *scientiae mechanicae* in philosophy. These constituted methodical reflections on specific remedies for bodily weakness – *lanificium* (weaving), *armatura* (metal work), *navigatio* (trade and transportation), *agricultura* (agriculture), *venatio* (perhaps primary sector activities would be a meaningful transposition), *medicina* and *theatrica* (entertainment). In each of these arts, Dindimus maintains, wisdom is hidden. Therefore, reflection on the art should be treated as a part of philosophy.

All living beings were born with the armor which befits them. Only man comes unarmed and naked into this world. What was given to others by birth, he must invent. Imitating nature and outfitting himself through reason, he shines forth more brightly than if he had been born with the equipment to cope with his environment.

Hugh manifests a deep cheerfulness, an intellectual optimism about human nature, which can only be appreciated when seen against the background of his medieval Christian faith. His theological writings show how fully he was imbued with the sense of human sinfulness and the need for redemption. He is equally convinced that human disobedience and aggression against nature were now forever reflected in nature's rebellion, nature's refusal to serve human desires and human needs. Yet he neither preaches resignation, nor does he incite us to submit nature to human domination. Rather, he sees in the man-caused disharmony between humans and their environment the critical challenge to humanity – the challenge to create artifacts which imitate nature, and which serve people as crutches on which they can rise above the condition in which they would have been had they lived on in Paradise. The study of the *wisdom* which is implicit in the construction of such crutches Hugh calls the mechanical sciences. And these he includes in philosophy.

A similar stance is taken by several contemporary proponents of science by people. They have no qualms about using the results of science *for* people, but claim that such use is for a purpose which is *sui generis*. To many, this claim sounds sentimental or fuzzy. And those who make it have no tradition of thought about science on which they can fall back. Perhaps reflection on Hugh of St. Victor can help them be more precise in their claims.

Hugh's originality in the treatment of the mechanical arts will be better understood by following the evolution of the term up to the end of the eleventh century. 'Mechanical' is of Greek origin (*mēchanē*). For the Greeks in classical times, the mechanical arts were procedures to outwit nature by miracles, magic, make-believe, by such technical devices as water clocks and parabolic mirrors. The same mechnical power became visible through gods, witches, actors and artisans. Later, when Greek became the trade language of the Mediterranean, *mēchanē* did the surprising things and *fabrica* did the straightforward. Latin never adopted the term, nor did it create an equivalent. The Roman genius did not need to outsmart nature. Roman builders were sure of their power: not even for that which we would call techniques did the Romans coin a catchall term. They could write with precision about agriculture or about the art of war (*de agricultura, de arte bellica*) – their own, that of others, or that which they brought to Rome. Their armies assembled techniques as they assembled gods in the Pantheon

But just as they had no need for theology, so they had no need for technology.

In late antiquity, the term *mēchanē* was rarely used. Before the Moors overran Spain, Isidore of Seville helped it, as so many other classical terms, to survive into the Middle Ages. For him mechanics meant any well thought-through process of 'making' for use or for the market. Then, at the time of Charlemagne, *artes mechanicae* acquired a new, ambiguous meaning. For the first time, scholars used the term explicitly to designate human activities through which artful imitations of nature were created. Gerber of Aurilac, the weird genius who became Pope Sylvester II, declared mechanical art to represent formulas describing the intricate movements of all the heavenly spheres. Simultaneously stone masons were said to use mechanical art to link the visible and the invisible world by the arrangements of apostles and dragons and flowers on the capitals of romanesque columns. Around the year 1000 *mechanica* was an élite term to designate a baffling power beyond that proper to priest or knight. This appears clearly from a letter which, around 830 an anonymous young monk wrote to Master E . . . (the name is illegible), his former teacher at the monastery of Compiègne:

. . . when I was with you, Master Manno told me what mechanics is all about, and what to think of the mechanical arts. Unfortunately, I have completely forgotten all this. Please find out and send me word – what are mechanical forces? And, above all, how does *mechanica* [magic] differ from *mathesis* [astrology]?

For the Greeks, the term had meant the outwitting of nature: for Hellenism something alike to competence, for the dark Middle Ages it meant a complement to astrology. In scholastic use at the time of Hugh, it meant making artful imitations of nature. It is in this sense that Hugh uses the word 'mechanical'. He explores the relations of practical art to wisdom.

Those who used the term in the Middle Ages before Hugh always combined it with art, writing of *artes mechanicae*. Hugh is alone in uniting it with science. He is the first to speak of *scientiae mechanicae*. He was concerned, not with wool making, but with the relationship between this art and wisdom. He dealt with spinning and weaving in a perspective not unlike that of Mahatma Gandhi. He wanted to establish the contribution which research about weaving or trading or medicine or acting would make to the scientist's wisdom, to his ability to remedy the weakness of his own being. In the practical arts, Hugh seeks a mirror of truth, as elsewhere he describes creation and the human soul as the other two great mirrors. And by the practice of the art, guided by science, he hopes to polish his mirror.

Analyzing art as a mirror for truth, Hugh establishes an essential difference between the reflection he sees in art and the one he sees in creation and the soul. Nature and the soul reflect the light of truth in a medium created by God albeit clouded by humans. The ecological aggression of the first couple disarrayed, but did not break these God-made mirrors. Mechanical science seeks the reflection of the same light in a medium made by the artist in the imitation of God's nature, a mirror which is partly natural and partly the work of man. Mechanical science is the study not of God's creation but of man's work insofar as this study can contribute to a practical remedy for human weakness.

Unlike the study of nature and man, the study of man's artifacts, Dindimus says, provides man with a pass-key to the workings of nature. To explain this two-faced, bastard quality of art, half human conception and half imitation of nature, Dindimus employs a preposterous etymology. He derives *mēchanē* from the Greek *moichos* (adulterer). For him, techniques mirror the truth, but also distort it: hence the scientific study of them, however truly philosophical, is a 'mechanical' or bastardly science.

Neither Hugh's idea of science as a remedy, nor his notion of mechanics as part of science, survived him. This is surprising, since both ideas are clearly expressed in the *Didascalicon*, his most popular work used as an introductory textbook well into the Renaissance. Part of the explanation as to why his readers did not take up these ideas is to be found in the accelerated technological developments which coincided with Hugh's 45 years of life. In less than a century, iron consumption in north-western Europe more than doubled. The iron was needed for such things as horseshoes, heavy ploughs and scythes – inventions three centuries old and only now widely used. And the Crusades began in this period, requiring large quantities of armor. In his lifetime the number of watermills doubled and the number and variety of new machines powered by these mills grew even faster. Monasteries appeared to be converted into machine parks. The men who built, maintained and repaired all this milling and mining equipment grew larger in number. They were the new kind of artisan and tradesman – wandering tinkerers and expert miners who did not quite fit former models. Now it was their trades that came to be called the mechanical arts. People tended to look down on the practitioners of such novel arts as a new kind of rabble. When, two generations after Hugh's death, both windmills and universities spread throughout Europe, no educated person would have talked about their trades or mechanics as an academic subject. The men designated as practicing mechanics were seen as a new kind of wage laborer – rare in twelfth century France – related to the first modern forms of mass production. The term 'mechanics' had by this time little to do with outwitting nature, and even less with its imitation. Its meaning was now closer to the exploitation of nature, having already evolved in the direction of its domination. Centuries would pass before any serious attempt would be made to incorporate disciplines which required manual skills into the university curriculum. Even medicine, when it entered the aula, had to exclude surgery. When, half a millenium later in the eighteenth century, finally the science of tool-construction found its way into the university curriculum, it was conceptualized as diametrically opposed to Hugh's *scientia mechanica* (science by people). Where the latter pursued wisdom in the imitation of nature, the new subject clearly was an *engineering* science: a science concerned with production for people.

The science of tools as tools has no proper name in English. 'Technology' will not do. This term is now used to speak about the tools themselves: a computer, bio-gas digester, machine park or the tool kit of some culture. In English, technology is also used to designate a subject. The civil, electronic or marine engineer is said to have received a technological formation. This English meaning of the term is now diffused throughout the globe. But until quite recently, this was not true in German or French. Jacques Ellul could quite legitimately distinguish techniques (which is what technology now means in English) from *la technologie* (the critical analysis of the relationship between people and tools). To be able to speak about this same matter, I propose the term, 'critical technology'.

When I was asked to write about science by people, I turned to the second quarter of the twelfth century because here, to the best of my knowledge, critical technology first made its appearance. And Hugh of St. Victor was not the only one of that period who had something to say about the relationship between tools and people. Honorius of Augsburg and Theophilus the Priest, for example, both made equally important contributions to the discussion. And I plan to write an essay on each, parallel to the present paper. In all cultures since antiquity, people have used tools, reported on their use and compared the effectiveness of one tool with another. And how-to-do-it manuals were common. Indian Brahmins, even more than Greek philosophers, critically analyzed the tools of thought used in logic and grammar. But no one in these instances explicitly and systematically turned the tools of manual labor into an issue of theoretical importance. Then around the year 1120, the tools of physical nature were for the first time recognized as a social or philosophical problem.

Hugh and the others who began to ask critical questions about techniques were themselves still rooted in cultures which took their tools for granted. In each of these cultures, the tool kit was limited. But from one culture to another, it was as diverse as the language. Further, new tools appeared from time to time and changed ways of living. For example, by the thirteenth century, the landscape of central Europe had been transformed due to a combination of tools which rendered the horse enormously more effective: the horseshoe, the bit, the collar and the deep plough. Meanwhile, other tools became obsolete. But even though tools changed, neither their transformation nor their social impact was seen as an issue for study.

Therefore, at the time of Hugh, it was still perfectly fitting to allow Dindimus the Brahmin to speak with a Christian mystic's voice of worldly wisdom. Christians still perceived the relationship between human beings and the environment in such a way, that conversation with a Taoist, Jew or Hindu could, in fact have started from common premises. No matter how effective or even destructive man's impact on the environment might be, people everywhere viewed agriculture as the maintenance of a former garden – however much threatened by weeds, insects or bad weather – and not as a form of biological mining. The improvement of tools, or the adoption of new ones, primarily raised yields or eased life rather than producing marketable surpluses.

In Hugh's generation, on the other hand, the signs of a profound change were appearing. The plough and the mill, for example, signified an increase in yields which went beyond the needs for subsistence, and the new city constituted a market where this surplus could be traded. A period of intense technical innovation and ecological aggression had started. In this setting, Hugh's ideas on mechanical science appeared: his theoretical insistence on the possibility of improving tools for subsistence, and his moral insistence that this ought to be the purpose of science.

By the end of the twelfth century, the climate of Europe had changed, both in the mechanical arts and in intellectual approaches. The differences between the great thinkers of the early twelfth and the early thirteenth centuries are often obscured when both are simply considered together as the 'scholastics'. Between the two groups, Spanish Jews and Benedictine monks translated the Greek philosophers from the Arabic manuscripts in which they had survived for 400 years. Then, an entirely new conception of science became general. Science came to be regarded as the search for what makes things tick rather than, as for Hugh, the caring pursuit of those remedies for the scientist's weakness which had been tasted by him and found pleasing. In the wake of this new approach to science a new attitude toward technical means came into being. The new mills became symbols of man's power over nature, the new clocks symbols of man's power over time. In fact, as C. S. Lewis remarks, the relationship turned out to be the power exercised by some men over others, with nature as the instrument. Critical technology, in Hugh's sense, ran counter to the passions and interests of the age, and was forgotten.

The critical technologist in 1130 and today are both on the

edge of a stage, but in very different ways. Hugh faced traditional naiveté, and we face its Baconian version. In Hugh's
world, a region's hoe and hammer were as much taken for
granted as its vernacular language and dress. When he observed
innovations, he proposed a theory according to which mechanical science improves the remedies for human weakness by
developing the art or by understanding the wisdom hidden in
it. In today's world, the critical technologist faces a different
form of naiveté, rooted in the formulations of Bacon.

Bacon, too, was concerned with theology, and preached more
than Hugh. He was interested in the ". . . restitution and re-
investiture of man to the sovereignty and power which he had
in his first state of creation in Paradise". For him, ". . . the
progress of arts and sciences [is] to achieve mastery over
nature"; the scientist comes to you, in ". . . very truth leading
to you Nature with all her children to bind you to her service
and make her your slave". He "vindicates the right over nature
. . . which is man's by divine bequest . . . [and] promises
liberation from the inconveniences of man's estate". Bacon
believed that ". . . the mechanical inventions of recent years do
not merely exert a gentle guidance over nature's course, they
have the power to conquer and to subdue her, to shake her to
her foundations".

Bacon proposed putting nature on the rack, torturing her by
experiment and thus forcing her to reveal her secrets. Now, in
the Seventies, Bacon has been made into a whipping boy. And,
although his style has gone out of fashion, his general optimism
remains intact. This can be well documented from contemporary ecology-oriented R & D. Such an endeavor seeks to
replace the domination of nature through torture by an alternative approach: the seduction of nature through blandishment.
Substantially, however, the new 'alternative' science very often
remains naive. It is generally an enterprise attempting to
liberate other people, indeed, all mankind, from the inconveniences of man's estate. It is a project undertaken by scientists
for the sake of other people. And increasingly, the new
ecologically-oriented R & D no longer pursues the production
of goods or services for more people. Rather, the research seeks
to determine what people have to be compelled to do for themselves, all the while believing that they do it for their own good.

From a science which attempts to control external nature, the new R & D has shifted toward the search for means which permit the subtle but effective imposition of self-control on people.

Unless science by people is based on critical technology, it is in serious trouble. It is in immediate danger of being absorbed by the R & D concerned with imposing prescribed forms of self-help on people. Just as Hugh's critical technology was forgotten – with his writings then serving as mere foundations for later scholastics – so science by people is in constant danger of being turned into a didactic tool of advanced ecology-oriented R & D. This cannot but happen unless we clearly recognize that science by people remains faithful to its task and purpose *only* when it starts from an image the inverse of man the worker and consumer, for whose sake specialists must do research.

V
SHADOW WORK

NADINE GORDIMER's novel *Burger's Daughter*, was on my desk as I began to outline this essay. With rare discipline, she reflects our age's liberal arrogance in the shameless, brilliant mirror of her homeland, the South African police state. Her protagonist suffers from an 'illness' – "not to be able to ignore that condition of a healthy, ordinary life: other people's suffering." In *The Feminization of America*, Ann Douglas makes a similar point. For her, the illness is the loss of sentimentality, a sentimentality asserting that the values which industrial society destroys are precisely those which it cherishes. There is no known substitute for this dishonesty in an industrial society. Those affected by the loss of sentimentality become aware of apartheid: that which we have now, or that which we shall get after the revolution.

In this essay, I want to explore why, in an industrial society, this apartheid is unavoidable; why without apartheid based on sex or pigmentation, on certification or race, or party membership, a society built on the assumption of scarcity cannot exist. And to approach the unexamined forms of apartheid in concrete terms, I want to speak about the fundamental bifurcation of work that is implicit in the industrial mode of production.

I have chosen as my theme the shady side of the industrial economy and, more specifically, the shady side of work. I do not mean badly paid work, nor unemployment; I mean unpaid work. The unpaid work which is unique to the industrial economy is my theme. In most societies men and women together have maintained and regenerated the subsistence of their households by unpaid activities. The household itself created most of what it needed to exist. These so-called subsistence activities are not my subject. My interest is in that entirely different form of unpaid work which an industrial society demands as a necessary complement to the production of goods and services. This kind of unpaid servitude does not contribute to subsistence. Quite the contrary, equally with wage labor, it ravages subsistence. I call this complement to wage labor 'shadow work'. It comprises most housework women do in their homes and apartments, the activities connected with shopping, most of the homework of students cramming for exams, the toil expended commuting to and from the job. It includes the stress of forced consumption, the tedious and regimented surrender to therapists, compliance with bureaucrats, the preparation for work to which one is compelled, and many of the activities usually labelled 'family life'.

In traditional cultures the shadow work is as marginal as wage labor, often difficult to identify. In industrial societies, it is assumed as routine. Euphemism, however, scatters it. Strong taboos act against its analysis as a unified entity. Industrial production determines its necessity, extent and forms. But it is hidden by the industrial-age ideology, according to which all those activities into which people are coerced for the sake of the economy, by means that are primarily social, count as satisfaction of needs rather than as work.

To grasp the nature of shadow work we must avoid two confusions. It is not a subsistence activity; it feeds the formal economy, not social subsistence. Nor is it underpaid wage labor; its unpaid performance is the condition for wages to be paid. I shall insist on the distinction between shadow and subsistence work, as much as on its distinction from wage labor, no matter how vigorous the protests from unionists, marxists and some feminists. I shall examine shadow work as a unique form of bondage, not much closer to servitude than to either slavery or wage labor.

While for wage labor you apply and qualify, to shadow work you are born or are diagnosed for. For wage labor you are selected; into shadow work you are put. The time, toil and loss of dignity entailed are exacted without pay. Yet increasingly the unpaid self-discipline of shadow work becomes more important than wage labor for further economic growth.

In advanced industrial economies these unpaid contributions toward economic growth have become the social locus of the most widespread, the most unchallenged, the most depressing form of discrimination. Shadow work, unnamed and un-examined, has become the principal area of discrimination against the majority in every industrial society. It cannot be ignored much longer. The amount of shadow work laid on a person today is a much better measure of discrimination than bias on the job. Rising unemployment and rising productivity combine now to create an increasing need to diagnose ever more people for shadow work. The 'age of leisure', the 'age of self-help', the 'service economy', are euphemisms for this grow-ing specter. To fully comprehend the nature of shadow work, I shall trace its history, a history which runs parallel to that of wage labor.

Both 'work' and 'job' are key words today. Neither had its present prominence three hundred years ago. Both are still un-translatable from European languages into many others. Most languages never had one single word to designate all activities that are considered useful. Some languages happen to have a word for activities demanding pay. This word usually connotes graft, bribery, tax or extortion of interest payments. None of these words would comprehend what we call 'work'.

For the last three decades, the Ministry for Language Development in Djakarta tried to impose the one term *bekerdja* in lieu of half a dozen others used to designate productive jobs. Sukarno had considered this monopoly of one term a necessary step for creating a Malay working class. The language planners got some compliance from journalists and union leaders. But the people continue to refer to what they do with different terms for pleasurable, or degrading, or tiresome, or bureaucratic actions – whether they are paid or not. All over Latin America, people find it easier to perform the paid task assigned to them than to grasp what the boss means by *trabajo*. For most toiling unem-ployed in Mexico, *desempleado* still means the unoccupied loafer on a well-paid job, not the unemployed whom the economist means by the term.

For classical Greeks or later Romans, work done with the hands, done under orders or involving income from trade was servile, better left to the lowly or slaves. In theory, Christians should have considered labor as part of each man's vocation. Paul, the tentmaker, had tried to introduce the Jewish work ethic into early Christianity: "who does not work shall not eat". In fact, though, this early Christian ideal was very thoroughly repressed. In Western monasteries, except for short periods of reform, the monks interpreted St. Benedict's motto 'ora et labora' as a call to supervise lay brothers at work, and to do God's work by prayer. Neither the Greeks nor the Middle Ages had a term resembling our work or job.

What today stands for work, namely, wage labor, was a badge of misery all through the Middle Ages. It stood in clear opposition to at least three other types of toil: the activities of the household by which most people subsisted, quite marginal to any money economy; the trades of people who made shoes, barbered or cut stones; the various forms of beggary by which people lived on what others shared with them. In principle, medieval society provided a berth for everyone whom it recognized as a member – its structural design excluded unemployment and destitution. When one engaged in wage labor, not occasionally as the member of a household but as a regular means of total support, he clearly signaled to the community that he, like a widow or an orphan, had no berth, no household, and so stood in need of public assistance.

In September of 1330 a rich cloth merchant died in Florence and left his property to be distributed among the destitute. The Guild of Or San Michele was to administer the estate. The 17,000 beneficiaries were selected and locked into the available churches at midnight. As they were let out, each received his inheritance. Now, how were these 'destitute' selected? We know, because we have access to the welfare notes of Or San Michele Guild in proto-industrial Florence. From it, we know the categories of the destitute: orphan, widow, victim of a recent act of God, heads of family totally dependent on wage work, or those compelled to pay rent for the roof over their bed. The need to provide for all the necessities of life by wage work was a sign of utter impotence in an age when poverty designated primarily a valued attitude rather than an economic condition. The pauper was opposed to the *potens*, the powerful, not yet to the *dives*, the rich. Until the late twelfth century, the term poverty designated primarily a realistic detachment from transitory things. The need to live by wage labor was the sign for the down and out, for those too wretched to be simply added to that huge medieval crowd of cripples, exiles, pilgrims, madmen, friars, ambulants, homeless that made up the world of the poor. The dependence on wage labor was the recognition that the worker did not have a home where he could contribute within the household. The right to beggary was a normative issue, but never the right to work.

To clarify the right to beggary, let me quote from a sermon by Ratger of Verona, preached nearly half a millenium earlier than the Florentine example. The sermon was delivered in 834 and is a moral exhortation on the rights and duties of beggars.

> You complain about your weakness. Rather thank God, do not complain, and pray for those who keep you alive. And you, over there, healthy though you are, complain about the burden of your large brood. Then abstain from your wife, but not without first getting her agreement, and work with your hands so that you can feed yourself and others. You say you cannot do this. Then cry about your own weakness, which is burdensome for you. Beg with restraint for what is necessary, abstain from all that is superfluous . . . Keep company with the sick, succor the dying and wash the dead.

Ratger here speaks about a right to beggary that for a thousand years was never challenged.

The abhorrence of wage labor still fits the outlook which might be shared by today's world majority. But with the current dominance of economics in everyday language, people lack the words to express their feelings directly. In a letter I received from a 23-year old Mexican, a kind of wonderment for those totally dependent on wage labor comes through clearly. Miguel is the son of a widow who brought up four children by growing radishes and selling them from a *petate* on the floor of the local market. Besides the children, there were always some outsiders eating or sleeping at her home. Miguel went to Germany as the guest of Mr. Mueller, a grade school teacher in his native village, who in five years had renovated part of an old house, adding a guest room. Miguel accepted the invitation in order to obtain training in art photography from Leitz. He wants to document traditional weaving techniques.

Unhampered by previous schooling, Miguel quickly learned to speak German. But he had difficulties understanding the people. In his letter, written after six months in Germany, he reported: "Señor Mueller behaves as *todo un senor* [a true gentleman might be the English equivalent]. But most Germans act like destitute people with too much money. No one can help another. No one can take people in – into his household." I believe that Miguel's comments reflect well the situation and attitudes of a past millenium: people who live on wages have no subsistent household, are deprived of the means to provide for their subsistence and feel impotent to offer any subsistence to others. For Miguel, wage labor has not yet gotten stuck beyond the looking glass.

But for most people in Europe and the West, wage labor went through the looking glass between the seventeenth and nineteenth century. Instead of being a proof of destitution, wages came to be perceived as a proof of usefulness. Rather than being a supplement to subsistent existence, wages came to be viewed – by those who paid them – as the natural source of livelihood for a population. These populations had been excluded from the means of subsistence by progressive forms of enclosures. An incident illustrates the beginning of this process. In 1777, barely twelve years before the Revolution, the Academy of Chalon-sur-Marne in Northwest France endowed a competition for the best treatment of the following problem: how to abolish rampant beggary in ways that would profit the Crown and be in the interest of the poor. The initiative reflects the increase of beggary in an age of enclosure, proto-industry and bourgeois values. It also reflects a new economic meaning of poverty, a condition now opposed, not to the powerful, but to the moneyed. The prize for the competition was awarded an essay whose opening sentences sum up its thesis: "For centuries, people have searched for the stone of wisdom. We have found it. It is work. Wage labor is the natural source of enrichment for the poor."

The author is certainly a man of letters, a clerk. He probably lives on some sinecure, a benefice or some other form of handout. To his own mental labors, he would never attribute such wondrous transforming powers. He would insist on his right to high-class beggary. He is a modern professor, who believes himself a white collar worker, justly earning his living, being socially productive. But for both, it would be true to say: those who since the eighteenth century write about work, its value, dignity, pleasures, always write about the work that others do.

The text also reflects the influence of hermetic or alchemic thought on social theory. Work is presented as the stone of wisdom, the panacea, the magic elixir which transforms what it touches into gold. Nature turns into priced goods and services by its contact with the labor which transmutes it. Making various concessions for the contribution of capital and resources to value, this is the fundamental position of classical economists from Adam Smith and Ricardo to Mill and Marx. The alchemic language of the late eighteenth century was replaced by Marx with the then fashionable 'coquetry', the language of chemistry. The hermetic perception of value has continued to determine the character of social ethics until today, even though the labor theory of value was replaced, in economics, first by utility theory, then by post-Keynesian thought, and finally by the utter confusion which attends the contemporary insight that "economists conceive of the world in terms that fail to grasp its essential characteristics or that seriously misrepresent them." Economists understand about work about as much as alchemists about gold.

The prize-winning essay of 1777 is also remarkable for the late date at which, in France, the policy to compel the poor to useful work was considered a novelty. Until the mid-eighteenth century, French poorhouses were run on the medieval Christian assumption that forced labor was a punishment for sin or crime. In protestant Europe and in some Italian cities which were industrialized early, that view had been abandoned a century earlier. The pioneering policies and equipment in Dutch Calvinist or North German workhouses clearly show this. They were organized and equipped for the cure of laziness and for the development of the will to do work as assigned. These workhouses were designed and built to transform useless beggars into useful workers. As such, they were the reverse of medieval alms-giving agencies. Set up to receive beggars caught by the police, these institutions softened them up for treatment by a few days of no food and a carefully planned ration of daily lashes. Then, treatment with work at the treadmill or at the rasp followed until the transformation of the inmate into a useful worker was diagnosed. One even finds provisions for intensive care. People resistant to work were thrown into a constantly flooding pit, where they could survive only by frantically pumping all day long. Not only in their pedagogical approach, but also in their method of training for self-approbation, these institutions are true precursors of compulsory schools. In 1612, only seventeen years after the foundation of the Amsterdam Workhouse, one of the regents published, tongue in cheek, a report on two dozen miraculous therapeutic successes. Each one purports to be the grateful acknowledgment of a cure from sloth by a successfully treated (schooled) patient. Even if these are authentic, they certainly do not reflect popular sentiment. The destitute of the eighteenth century, by this date generally labelled as the 'poor', violently resisted such efforts to qualify them for work. They sheltered and defended those whom the police tried to classify as 'beggars' and whom the government tried to cure of social uselessness in order to protect the unobtrusive poor from such vagrants.

Even the harshest governments seemed unsuccessful in their forays. The crowd remained ungovernable. The Prussian Secretary of the Interior, in 1747, threatens severe punishment to anyone who interferes with the poverty-police:

> . . . from morning till night, we try to have this police cruise through our streets to stop beggary . . . but as soon as soldiers, commoners or the crowd notice the arrest of a beggar to bring him to the poorhouse, they riot, beat up our officers sometimes hurting them grievously and liberate the beggar. It has become almost impossible to get the poverty-police to take to the street . . .

Seven more analogous decrees were issued during the following thirty years.

All through the eighteenth and well into the nineteenth century, the project of Economic Alchemy produced no echo from below. The plebeians rioted. They rioted for just grain prices, they rioted against the export of grain from their regions, they rioted to protect prisoners of debt and felt protected whenever the law seemed not to coincide with their tradition of natural justice. The proto-industrial plebian crowd defended its 'moral economy' as Thompson has called it. And they rioted against the attacks on this economy's social foundation: against the enclosure of sheep and now against the enclosure of beggars. And in these riots, the crowd was led, more often than not, by its women. How did this rioting proto-industrial crowd, defending its right to subsistence turn into a striking labor force, defending 'rights' to wages? What was the social device that did the job, where the new poor laws and workhouses had failed? It was the economic division of labor into a productive and a non-productive kind, pioneered and first enforced through the domestic enclosure of women.

An unprecedented economic division of the sexes, an unprecedented economic conception of the family, an unprecedented antagonism between the domestic and public spheres made wage work into a necessary adjunct of life. All this was accomplished by making working men into the wardens of their domestic women, one on one, and making this guardianship into a burdensome duty. The enclosure of women succeeded where the enclosure of sheep and beggars had failed.

Why the struggle for subsistence was so suddenly abandoned and why this demise went unnoticed, can be understood only by bringing to light the concurrent creation of shadow work and the theory that woman, by her scientifically discovered nature, was destined to do it. While men were encouraged to revel in their new vocation to the working class, women were surreptitiously redefined as the ambulant, full-time matrix of society. Philosophers and physicians combined to enlighten society about the true nature of woman's body and soul. This new conception of her 'nature' destined her for activities in a kind of home which discriminated against her wage labor as effectively as it precluded any real contribution to the household's subsistence. In practice, the labor theory of value made man's work into the catalyst of gold, and degraded the homebody into a housewife economically dependent and, as never before, unproductive. She was now man's beautiful property and faithful support needing the shelter of home for her labor of love.

The bourgeois war on subsistence could enlist mass support only when the plebeian rabble turned into a clean-living working class made up of economically distinct men and women. As a member of this class, the man found himself in a conspiracy with his employer – both were equally concerned with economic expansion and the suppression of subsistence. Yet this fundamental collusion between capital and labor in the war on subsistence was mystified by the ritual of class struggle. Simultaneously man, as head of a family increasingly dependent on his wages, was urged to perceive himself burdened with all society's legitimate work, and under constant extortion from an unproductive woman. In and through the family the two complementary forms of industrial work were now fused: wage work and shadow work. Man and woman, both effectively estranged from subsistence activities, became the motive for the other's exploitation for the profit of the employer and investments in capital goods. Increasingly, surplus was not invested only in the so-called means of production. Shadow work itself became more and more capital-intensive. Investments in the home, the garage and the kitchen reflect the disappearance of subsistence from the household, and the evidence of a growing monopoly of shadow work. Yet this shadow work has been consistently mystified. Four such mystifications are still current today.

The first comes masked as an appeal to biology. It describes the relegation of women to the role of mothering housewives as a universal and necessary condition to allow men to hunt for the prey of the job. Four modern disciplines seem to legitimate this assumption. Ethologists describe female apes like housewives guarding the nest, while the males hunt through the trees. From this projection of family roles onto the ape, they infer that nesting is the gender specific role of the female and real work, that is, the conquest of scarce resources, is the task of the male. The myth of the mighty hunter is then by them defined as a cross-cultural constant, a behavioral bedrock of humanoids, derived from some biological substratum of higher mammals. Anthropologists irresistibly rediscover among savages the traits of their own moms and dads, and find features of the apartments in which they were bred, in tents, huts and caves. From hundreds of cultures, they gather evidence that women were always handicaped by their sex, good for digging rather than hunting, guardians of the home. Sociologists, like Parsons, start from the functions they believe to discern in today's family and then let the gender-roles within the family illuminate the other structures of society. Finally, sociobiologists of the right and the left give a contemporary veneer to the enlightenment myth that female behavior is male adaptive.

Common to all these is a basic confusion between the gender-specific assignment of tasks that is characteristic for each culture, and the uniquely modern economic bifurcation in nineteenth century work ideology that establishes a previously unknown apartheid between the sexes: he, primarily the producer; she, primarily private-domestic. This economic distinction of sex-roles was impossible under conditions of subsistence. It uses mystified tradition to legitimate the growing distinction of consumption and production by *defining what women do as non-work*.

The second mask for shadow work confuses it with 'social reproduction'. This latter term is an unfortunate category that Marxists use to label sundry activities which do not fit their ideology of work, but which must be done by someone – for example, keeping house for the wage worker. It is carelessly applied to what most people did most of the time in most societies, that is, subsistence activities. Also, it named activities that in the late nineteenth century were still considered to be non-productive wage labor, the work of teachers or social workers. Social reproduction includes most of what all people do around the home today. The label thus thwarts every attempt to grasp the difference between woman's basic and vital contribution to a subsistence economy, and her unpaid conscription into the reproduction of industrial labor – *unproductive women are consoled with 're-production'*.

The third device that masks shadow work is the assignment of shadow prices to sundry behavior outside the monetary market. All unpaid activities are amalgamated into a so-called informal sector. While the old economists built their theory on the foregone conclusion that every commodity consumption implied the satisfaction of a need, the new economists go further: for them, every human decision is the evidence of a satisfying preference. They build economic models for crime, leisure, learning, fertility, discrimination and voting behavior. Marriage is no exception. Gary S. Becker, for instance, starts from the assumption of a sex-market in equilibrium, and hence derives formulas that describe the 'division of outputs between mates'. Others calculate the value added by the housewife to a TV dinner made by her unpaid activities in selecting, heating and serving it. Potentially, this line of thought would permit to argue that wage workers would be better off if they were to live as homebodies, that capital accumulation is what women have been doing unpaid at home. For Milton Friedman's pupils, *it is sex which offers a paradigm for the economics of what women do.*

A fourth mask is placed on shadow work by the majority of feminists writing on housework. They know that it is hard work. They fume because it is unpaid. Unlike most economists, they consider the wages lost huge, rather than trifling. Further, some of them believe that women's work is 'non-productive' and yet the main source of the "mystery of primitive accumulation", a contradiction that had baffled omniscient Marx. They add feminist sunshades to Marxist spectacles. They wed the house-wife to a wage-earning patriarch whose pay, rather than his penis, is the prime object of envy. They do not seem to have noticed that the redefinition of woman's nature after the French Revolution went hand in hand with that of man's. They are thus double blind both to the nineteenth century conspiracy of class enemies at the service of growth and to its reinforcement by the twentieth century war for the economic equality of the sexes they carry into each home. Abstract sex-roles in society at large rather than real pants in the home have become the issue of the domestic battle. The woman-oriented outlook of these feminists has helped them to publicize the degrading nature of unpaid work is now added to discrimination on the job, but their movement-specific commitment has compelled them to cloud the key issue: the fact that modern women are crippled by being compelled to labor that, in addition to being un-salaried in economic terms, is fruitless in terms of subsistence.

Recently, however, some new historians of women's work have penetrated beyond conventional categories and approaches. They refuse to view their subject through hand-me-down professional glasses choosing rather to look from 'below the belt'. They study childbirth, breastfeeding, housecleaning, prostitution, rape, dirty laundry and speech, mother's love, child-hood, abortion, menopause. They have revealed how gyneco-logists, architects, druggists and colleagues in chairs of history reached into this disorderly grab bag to create symptoms and market novel therapies. Some of them unravel the home life of third world women in the new urban slums, and contrast it with the life in the *campo* or *kampung*. Others explore the 'labor of love' which was invented for women in neighborhoods, clinics and political parties.

The pathfinding innovators who dare to view industrial society from its shady and messy underside light up and dissect kinds of oppression heretofore hidden. What they then report does not fit the available -isms and -ologies. Not looking at the effects of industrialization from above, their findings turn out to be quite other than the pinnacles which managers describe, than the crevices which workers feel, than the principles which ideologues impose. And their eyes see differently than the ethno-anthropological explorers who are more accustomed through their training to view the Zande or to reconstruct a village priest's life in medieval Provence. Such unconventional research now violates a long-standing scholarly and political double taboo – the shadow which hides the Siamese twin nature of industrial work, and the prohibition to seek new terms to describe it.

Unlike the suffragettes of the social sciences, who seem obsessed by what enclosure has 'unjustly' denied them, the historians of female intimacy recognize that housework is *sui generis*. of its own kind They detect the spread of a new shadow existence between 1780 and 1860, in different countries at a different rhythm. They report on a new life whose frustrations are not less painful when they are, occasionally, artfully guilded. They describe how this *sui generis* work was exported, together with wage labor, beyond the confines of Europe. And they observe that, wherever women became second best on the labor market, their work, when unpaid, was profoundly changed. Parallel with second-class wage work organized for women, first at the sewing machine, then at the typewriter and finally on the telephone, something new, the disestablished housewife came into being.

This transmogrification of housework is particularly obvious in the United States because it happened so abruptly. In 1810 the common productive unit in New England was still the rural household. Processing and preserving of food, candlemaking, soapmaking, spinning, weaving, shoemaking, quilting, rugmaking, the keeping of small animals and gardens, all took place on domestic premises. Although money income might be obtained by the household through the sale of produce, and additional money be earned through occasional wages to its members, the United States household was overwhelmingly self-sufficient. Buying and selling, even when money did change hands, was often conducted on a barter basis. Women were as active in the creation of domestic self-sufficiency as were men. They brought home about the same salaries. They still were, *economically*, men's equals. In addition, they usually held the pursestrings. And further, they were as actively engaged in feeding, clothing and equipping the nation during the turn of the century. In 1810, in North America, twenty-four out of twenty-five yards of wool were of domestic origin. This picture had changed by 1830. Commercial farming had begun to replace subsistence farms. The living wage had become common, and dependence on occasional wage work began to be seen as a sign of poverty. The woman, formerly the mistress of a household that provided sustenance for the family, now became the guardian of a place where children stayed before they began to work, where the husband rested, and where his income was spent. Ann Douglas has called this transmogrification of women their 'disestablisment'. In fact, it strongly suggests the epoch's clerical aspirations and anxieties. Just as the clergyman of the time had been newly segregated in a strictly ecclesiastic realm, women were now both flattered and threatened to stick to their proper sphere where lip-service could be paid to the superiority of their functions. With their economic equality, women lost many of their legal privileges, among them the right to vote. They vanished from traditional trades, were replaced by male obstetricians in midwifery, and found the way into the new professions barred. Their economic disestablishment reflected society's commitment to the satisfaction of basic needs in the home by means of products created in wage labor that had moved away from the household. Deprived of subsistence, marginal on the labor market, the frustrating task of the housewife became the organization of compulsory consumption. The existence which is becoming typical of men and children in the 1980's was already well-known to a growing number of women in the 1850's.

The new historians of female sensitivity and mentality ostensibly concentrate on women's work. But, in fact, they have given us the first coherent report written by trained historians who speak as losers in the war against subsistence. They provide

us a history of 'work' performed in the shadow of economic
searchlights, written by those who are compelled to do it. This
shadow, of course, blights much more than motherly or wifely
duties. It infallibly extends with progress and spreads with the
development of the economic sphere, reaching further into both
men's and women's lives to leave no one's day completely un-
clouded. The housewife will probably remain forever as the icon
of this shadow existence, just as the man in overalls will survive
the microprocessor as the icon of the 'industrial worker'. But to
make this other half of industrial existence into women's work,
tout court, would be the fifth and ultimate mystification. It would
forever besmirch the personal reality of women with a sex invented for economic control. For this reason, I propose 'shadow
work' to designate a social reality whose prototype is modern
housework. Add the rising number of unemployed to the increasing number of people kept on the job only to keep
them busy, and it becomes obvious that shadow work is by
far more common in our late industrial age than paid jobs.
By the end of the century, the productive worker will be the
exception.

Shadow work and wage labor came into existence together.
Both alienate equally, though they do so in profoundly different
ways. Bondage to shadow work was first achieved primarily
through economic sex-coupling. The nineteenth century bourgeois family made up of the wage earner and his dependents
replaced the subsistence-centered household. It tied the *femina
domestica* and a *vir laborans* in the thraldom of complementary
impotence typical for *homo economicus*. This crude model of bondage to shadow work could not suffice for economic expansion:
profits for capitalists are derived from compulsory consumers
just as the power of professionals and bureaucrats is derived
from disciplined clients. Both capitalists and commisars profit
more from shadow work than from wage labor. The sex-
coupling family provided them with a blueprint for more complex and more subtly disabling forms of bondage to shadow
work. This bondage today is effected essentially through social
agents empowered for diagnosis. Diagnosis literally means discrimination, knowing-apart. It is used today to designate the
act by which a profession defines you as its client. Whatever
allows a profession to impute a need for dependence on its

services will do quite well to impose the corresponding shadow work on the client. Medical scientists and pedagogues are typical examples of such disabling professions. They impose the shadow work of service consumption on their clients and get paid for it out of the clients' income, either directly or through taxed monies. In this fashion, the modern professionals who produce care push the pattern of the work-bonding modern family one step further: through wage labor, people in 'caring relationship' jobs now produce precisely those frustrating things which women in the nineteenth century family were originally compelled to do or make for no pay whatever. The creation of professionally supervised shadow work has become society's major business. Those paid to create shadow work are today's élite. As housework is only the most visible tip of shadow labor so the gynecological engineering of the housewife is only the most impudent cover for society-wide diagnostics. For example, the sixteen levels of relative degradation which define the classes of dropouts from the educational system assign disproportionate burdens of shadow work to society's lower and larger cohorts, and do so much more subtly than sex or race ever could have done.

The discovery of shadow work could well be, for the historian, as important as the discovery – a generation ago – of popular cultures and peasants as subjects of history. Then Karl Polanyi and the great Frenchmen around the *Annales* pioneered the study of the poor, of their ways of life, their sensibilities and world views. They brought the subsistence of the weak and illiterate into the realm of historical research. The study of women under the impact of industrialization can be understood as a beachhead into another no-man's-land of history: the forms of life that are typical only to industrial society yet remain invisible, as long as this society is studied under the assumptions about scarcity, desire, sex or work that it has secreted. The discovery of this shadow realm, which is distinct both from that of subsistent popular cultures and from that of political and social economy, will make those whom André Gorz calls 'post-proletarians' into subjects of history. And the historian will be able to see that the diagnostic procedure that first dis-established women by opposing them to men, in the meantime has dis-established everyone in multiple ways. In this perspective, the history of the industrial age is that of a radically new kind of discrimination.

This 'civil' war against popular cultures and vernacular values could never have succeeded unless those to be divested of subsistence had first accepted their enclosure into distinct spheres and thereby had been divided. The creation of the housewife bespeaks an unprecedented, a sexual apartheid. But it also illustrates the kind of consciousness in which desire could not but become mimetic. The many attempts to make this dividing line appear as a prolongation of traditional frontiers that have forever separated people from people, is as futile as the attempt to make industrial work appear as a prolongation of what people always did – both serve the same mystification. Both protect the taboo that covers the unexamined life of our age. People who insist on interpreting the current status of women as updated purdah must miss the point. Equally, those who view relegation to South African Homelands as a modern resettlement based on traditional attitudes toward distinct pigmentation totally miss the meaning of the color line. And anyone who sees the zek in the gulag primarily as a slave is blind to the motto that only a Hitler presumed to write large on the entrance to Auschwitz: "Arbeit macht frei". He will never understand a society in which the unpaid work of the Jew in the camp is exacted from him as his due contribution to his own extinction. Modern enclosure, apartheid, is never just cruel or just degrading, it has always a demonic dimension. Prose cannot do justice to a social organization set up to enlist people in their own destruction. To grasp its meaning we have to listen to the *Todesfuge* of Paul Celan, ". . . und sie schaufeln ein Grab in den Lüften . . . ein Grab in den Wolken, da liegt man nicht eng". The subtler forms of apartheid can blur our vision for the *mysterium iniquitatis* always inherent in them. Yesterday's fascism in Germany, or today's in South Africa manifest it.

Industrial society cannot forgo its victims. Nineteenth century women were enclosed, dis-established, they were damaged. Inevitably they had a corrupting influence on society at large. They provided that society with an object for *sentimental* compassion. Oppression always forces its victims to do society's dirty work. Our society forces its victims to become cooperative objects of oppression through care. Its condition for ordinary happiness is sentimental concern for others that ought to be helped, saved or liberated. This is the story that Nadine Gordimer told me, not about women, not about pupils, patients or inmates, but about blacks. She told it to me with "the deceptive commonplace that people, accustomed to police harassment, use before the uninitiated", an attitude that she attributes to her main character, Burger's daughter. For her there is no ordinary happiness, because she is ill. The illness that she describes is the loss of that sentimentalism on which ordinary happiness today depends.

Ann Douglas, the American, has well described this sentimentalism. It is a complex phenomenon that in industrial societies is the substratum of ideologies and religions. It asserts that the values that an industrial society's activities deny are precisely those that it cherishes. It asserts that the values now attributed to subsistence – subsistence which economic growth inevitably destroys – are precisely those for the sake of which growth must continue. It transmogrifies subsistence into the economy's shadow. Sentimentalism succeeds in dealing with the apartheid, implicit in the opposition between production and consumption, by manipulating nostalgia for subsistence. And this 'subsistence' to which nostalgia aspires, turns out to be the economy's shadow which is the converse of the vernacular domain. The sentimental glorification of the victims of apartheid: women, patients, blacks, illiterates, the underdeveloped, addicts, the underdog, the proletariat, provides a way to solemnly protest a power to which one has already capitulated. This sentimentalism is a dishonesty for which there is no known substitute in a society that has ravished its own environment for subsistence. Such a society depends on ever new diagnoses of those for whom it must care. And this paternalistic dishonesty enables the representatives of the oppressed to seek power for ever new oppression.

NOTES AND BIBLIOGRAPHIES

NOTES ON 'THE WAR AGAINST SUBSISTENCE'

In connection with my comments on Nebrija, consult for further readings on the history of taught mother tongue:

HEISING, Karl, Muttersprache, ein romanistischer Beitrag zur Genesis eines deutschen Wortes und zur Erstehung der deutsch-franzoesischen Sprachgrenze, in: *Mundartforschung*, XXIII, 3, pp. 144–174.

DAUBE, Anna, *Der Aufstieg der Muttersprache im deutschen Denken des 15. und 16. Jahrhunderts*, Deutsche Forschungen, Vol. 34, Verlag Diesterweg, 1940. A mediocre doctoral thesis, but a repository of quotations.

BOSSONG, Georg, *Probleme der Uebersetzung wissenschaftlicher Werke aus dem Arabischen in das Altspanische zur Zeit Alfonsos des Weisen*, Niemeyer Verlag, Tuebingen, 1979.

AUERBACH, Erich, *Literatursprache und Publikum in der lateinischen Spaetantike und im Mittelalter*, Francke Verlag, Berlin. Especially Chapter IV.

TANLA-KISHANI, Bongasu, African Cultural Identity through Western Philosophies and Languages, in: *Présence Africanie 98*, second trimester 1967, p. 127. "The ordinary man on the streets of Africa can at times be led to think that one is only bilingual when one can manipulate two European languages, since African languages are graded as dialects, vernacular, patois."

JOSTEN, Dirk, Sprachvorbild und Sprachnorm im Urteil des 16, und 17. Jahrhunderts. Sprachlandschaftliche Prioritaeten, Sprachautoritaeten, Sprachimmanente Argumentation, in: *Europaeische Hochschulschriften*, R 1, 152, Bern/Frankfurt, Lang, 1976. Gives the contemporary opinions of German thinkers.

BAHNER, W., Beitraege zum Sprachbewusstsein in der spanischen Literatur des 16. und 17. Jahrhunderts, Berlin, Ruettner Verlag, 1956.

GUIDE TO THE STUDY OF HUGH OF ST. VICTOR AND THE MECHANICAL SCIENCES

THIS essay is based on one of twelve lectures offered at Kassel, Germany, during the 1979–80 winter semester. The purpose of the lectures was to sharpen the students' awareness of the limitations in contemporary thought and feeling which make a real understanding of subsistence-oriented cultures well-nigh impossible. The method used was to confront students with medieval texts selected principally from the second quarter of the twelfth century.

The essay was then written for a totally different purpose, to appear in a reader edited by Valentina Borremans. There it will be printed with essays by Karl Polanyi, Lewis Mumford, André Gorz, and others, all concerned with the radical criticism of tools. As an appendix to this volume, Borremans' *Guide to Convivial Tools* will be reprinted. This work includes more than 450 modern reference tools dealing with science or technology by people.

The following guide to the study of Hugh of St. Victor and the mechanical arts in the Middle Ages is not provided to back up the statements of my essay. Rather, it is an invitation extended to some unknown reader, possessing a general knowledge of medieval history, who wishes to explore those of my remarks which strike him or her as worthwhile.

Biography: J. TAYLOR, The Origin and Early Life of Hugh of St. Victor: an evaluation of the tradition. Notre Dame (Indiana) 1957. 70 pp. (Texts and

Studies in the History of Medieval Education vol. 5).

Texts: Opera Omnia. Vol. 1–3. Paris 1854–79 (Migne, Patrologia Latina vol. 175–77).

Opera propaedeutica. Practica geometriae. De grammatica, Epitome Dindimi in philosophiam. Ed. R. BARON. Notre Dame (Indiana) 1966. 247 pp. (University of Notre Dame Publications in Medieval Studies 20). Note: pp. 167–207 give the Latin critical text of the Dialogue with Dindimus, pp. 209–47 fifty explanatory notes by the editor.

Didascalicon de studio legendi. A critical text. Ed. by C. H. BUTTIMER. Washington 1939. 160 pp. (The Catholic University Press, Studies in Medieval and Renaissance Latin vol. 10.) The English edition of this text brings the critical apparatus and the notes added in the introduction up to a later date: The Didascalicon of Hugh of St. Victor. A medieval guide to the arts. Translated from the Latin with an introduction and Notes by J. TAYLOR, New York, London (1961) (Records of civilization, sources and studies.)

His thought: R. BARON, since his doctoral thesis in 1957 has written a dozen contributions through which Hugh of St. Victor can be understood in an entirely new way. His doctoral thesis deals with Science and Wisdom in Hugh: Science et sagesse chez H. de S.V. Paris, Lethielleu 1957 (complete bibliography pp. 231–63) is the best introduction. M. GRABMANN, Hugo von St. Victor und Peter Abelard. *Ein Gedenkblatt zum 800 jaehr. Todestag zweier Denkergestalten des Mittelalters,* in: Theologie und Glaube 34 (1942) pp. 241–9.

E. LICCARO, L'Uomo e la natura nel pensiero di Ugo di S.V. in Atti del 3. Congresso internazionale di filosofia medievale, Milano 1966 pp. 305–13. B. Lacroix, *H. de S.V. et les conditions du savoir au moyen age,* in: An E. Gilson Tribute,

Milwaukee 1959 (Marquette University Studies) pp. 118–34.

Dictionary art: Both excellent for a first orientation: DICTIONNAIRE DE SPIRITUALITE, Beauchesne Paris 1969, *art* H. de St. V. by R. BARON and DICTIONNAIRE DE THEOLOGIE CATHOLIQUE, Lethouzey, 1930, *art:* H. de S.-V. by F. VERNET.

Originality of Hugh's Concept of Remedy: L. M. DE RIJK, Some Notes on the Twelfth Century Topic of the Three (Four) Human Evils and of Science, Virtue and Techniques as their Remedies, in: VIVARIUM, Leiden, 5 (1967) pp. 8–15. Collates the known twelfth-century texts and compares them.

Originality of Hugh's Division of the Sciences: Bernard BISCHOFF, *Eine verschollene Einteilung der Wissenschaften* in: Archives d'Histoire Doctrinale et Littéraire du Moyen Age 25 (1959) pp. 5–20. & D. Luigi CALONGHI, La scienza e la classificazione delle scienze in Ugo di S. Vitore. Estratto della dissertazione di Laurea. Pontificium Athenaeum Salesianum. Facultas philosophica. Theses ad Lauream Nr 41, Torino 1956 (1957).

On the Place of the Mechanical Arts in Medieval Thought the two major monographs are: Peter STERNAGEL, Die artes mechanicae im Mittelalter: Begriffs- und Bedeutungsgeschichte bis zum Ende des 13. Jahrhunderts. Lassleben, Kallmuetz 1966 (Muenchner Historische Studien, Abteilung Mittelalterliche Geschichte, Vol. 2) on Hugh pp. 67–77; on his influence pp. 85–102. Franco ALESSIO, La filosofia e le artes mechanicae nel secolo 12, in Studi Medievali 3rd series v 6 (1965) pp. 71–161. On the Relation to Servile Work: M. D. CHENU, *Arts mecaniques et oeuvres serviles* in: Revue des sciences philosophiques et theologiques 29 (1940) pp. 313–15.

Hugo and the History of the Engineering Curriculum: WHITE, Lynn Jr. *Medieval Engineering and the Sociology of Knowledge* in: Pacific Historical Review 44 (1975) pp. 1–21. This article led me to read Hugh, with whom I was mainly acquainted as an analyst of mystical experience, to find out about his teachings on mechanical science. Like every article of White I know, this too was a sure guide to the secondary literature on its subject. White stresses the fact that for centuries after Hugh, the teaching of mechanics within the University Curriculum was never again seriously envisaged. I tried to stress the complementary point: never again, until this decade, was the teaching of mechanical science envisaged as a *remedium* of human weakness, as one of the roads that lead their student to *comodum*, ease in face of physical reality, as *theorica* lead him to science in the sense of wisdom, and *practica* to virtue.

READINGS TO 'SHADOW WORK'

The text of shadow work was written for delivery as a speech. Several people have begun to use it as an outline for their studies. At their request I here publish extracts from my own working bibliography. I arranged my comments under headings which roughly correspond to the successive arguments developed in the speech.

The History of Scarcity

Economics always implies the assumption of scarcity. What is not scarce cannot be subjected to economic control. This is as true of goods and services, as it is of work. The assumption of scarcity has penetrated all modern institutions. Education is built on the assumption that desirable knowledge is scarce. Medicine assumes the same about health, transportation about time, and unions about work. The modern family itself is built on the assumption that productive activities are scarce. This assumption of scarcity, rather than the nuclear, conjugal organization of the household, distinguishes the modern family from that of other times. The identification of that which is desirable with that which is scarce has deeply shaped our thinking, our feeling, our perception of reality itself. Scarcity that in other societies colored a few well defined values – such as foodstuffs in spring and war-time, arable land, pepper or slaves – now seems to affect all values of public concern. Being thus immersed in it, we have become blind to the paradox that scarcity increases in a society with the rise of the GNP. This kind of scarcity which we take for granted was – and largely still is – unknown outside of commodity-intensive societies. The history of this sense of scarcity, however, still remains to be written.

A major step toward such a history has been made in 1979 by Paul Dumouchel and Jean-Pierre Dupuy in the two separate essays they published under the joint title *L'enfer des choses*. Both authors start with an insight to which they were helped by René Girard. Girard, a Frenchman, demonstrated in 1961 that the great novelists of the nineteenth century had made a discovery that consistently has eluded the social scientists. These novelists describe a radical mutation of human desire and of envy. This transformation can be observed already in *Don Quixote* of Cervantes, but it becomes pervasive in the time of Dostoyevsky. In Girard's words, these bourgeois novelists were aware of the fact that desire, that in other previous literature had a direct object, becomes in the nineteenth century triangular, mimetic. The protagonists of the great novelists live in a society that has made it almost impossible to desire, except what others, whom one envies, either have or want. And when these protagonists pursue their desires in this fashion, they transmogrify their envy into virtue. When they imitate their model, they believe that they do so to distinguish themselves from it. Guided by Girard, the two authors, Dumouchel and Dupuy, locate the uniqueness of modern institutions in the institutional arrangements that foster mimetic desire and, with it, scarcity of an unprecedented kind. Instead of using Marx, Freud or Lévi-Strauss to demystify Dostoyevsky, they demystify the great political economists, psychoanalists and structuralists who, each in different ways, spin their yarn out of a historical scarcity. They expose scarcity that is defined by mimetic desire as the foregone conclusion on which the entire edifice of commodity-intensive economics is built.

Bibliography on 'mimetic desire': the modernization of envy

The thesis is stated in GIRARD, René, *Mensonge romantique et vérité romanesque*, Paris: Grasset, 1961. (Engl. ed. *Deceit, Desire and the Novel: Self and Other in Literary Structure*. Transl. by Yvonne Freccero, Johns Hopkins, 1976). The later book: GIRARD, René, *La violence et le sacré*, Paris: Grasset, 1972. (Engl.

Violence and the Sacred. Transl. by Patrick Gregory, Johns Hopkins, 1977) is crucial for understanding DUMOUCHEL, Paul and DUPUY, Jean-Pierre, *L'enfer des choses*, Paris: Seuil, 1979. Some readers will find it easier to begin this book with the second essay by Dumouchel, and then read the first by Dupuy. The latter, Dupuy, begins his argument with a commentary on FOSTER, George M., 'The Anatomy of Envy: A Study in Symbolic Behavior', in: *Current Anthropology*, Vol. 13, no. 2, April 1972, pp. 165–202. This essay contains an excellent bibliography and short comments by three dozen social scientists to whom it was sent before publication.

For the history of the perception of envy in classical antiquity, the following can be recommended: RANULF, Svend, *The Jealousy of the Gods and Criminal Law in Athens*, transl. Annie J. Fausböll, 2 vols. Copenhagen: Levin and Munksgaard, 1933–34. On Hybris calling for Nemesis: GRENE, David, *Greek Political Theory: The Image of Man in Thucydides and Plato*, Chicago: Univ. of Chicago Press, Phoenix Books, 1965. (orig. *Man in His Pride*), and DODDS, E. R., *The Greeks and the Irrational*, Berkeley: Univ. of California Press, 1951, especially chap. 2. For an orientation of the medieval understanding of envy, see: RANWEZ, Edouard, 'Envie', in: *Dictionnaire de Spriritualité*, cols. 774–85; VINCENT-CASSY, Mireille, *Quelques réflexions sur l'envie et la jalousie en France au XIV° siècle*, in: MOLLAT, *Etudes*, II, pp. 487–504; and LITTLE, Lester, 'Pride goes Before Avarice: Social Change and the Vices in Latin Christendom', in: *The American Historical Review*, no. 76, 1971, pp. 16–49.

Since Freud first postulated an inborn female envy for what standard English, from the sixteenth to the eighteenth century called 'the tool' (see OED), discussion about envy has turned psychoanalytic. KLEIN, Melanie, *Envy and Gratitude*, Delacorte Press, 1975, especially pp. 176–235. See also: SCHOECK, Helmut, *A Theory of Social Behavior*, New York: Harcourt, Brace & World, 1970. Orig. *Der Neid und die Gesellschaft*, Freiburg: Herder, 4th ed. 1974.

For a medieval understanding of envy, its opposite would have to be understood: GAUTHIER, R.-A., *Magnanimité: L'idéal de la grandeur dans la philosophie païenne et dans la théologie chrétienne*, Paris: Vrin, 1951, amply studies the transition from classical to Christian magnanimity. See also LADNER, Gerhard, 'Greatness in Medieval History', in: *The Catholic Historical Review*, Vol. L, no. 1, April 1964, pp. 1–26. McCAWLEY, J. D., 'Verbs of Bitching', in: HOCKNEY, D. ed., *Contemporary Research in Philosophical Logic and Linguistic Semantics*, pp. 313–32, has whetted my appetite for semantic studies on the history of envy in contemporary languages.

Bibliography on commodity-intensive versus subsistence 'economies'

I have adopted the term 'commodity-intensive society' from LEISS, William, *The Limits to Satisfaction*, London: Boyars, 1978. In the introduction to this British edition the author defines his own position relative to five other recent books that deal with the same subject in different ways: "... Robert Heilbroner, *Business Civilisation in Decline*; Stuart Ewen, *Captains of Consciousness: Advertising and the Social Roots of the Consumer Culture*; Tibor Scitovsky, *The Joyless Economy: An Inquiry into Human Satisfaction and Consumer Dissatisfaction*; Fred Hirsch, *Social Limits to Growth*; and Marshall Sahlins, *Culture and Practical Reason*." LEISS, William, *The Domination of Nature*, New York: Braziller, 1972, is fundamental.

To prepare for a discussion of the historical uniqueness of a disembedded economy typical for industrial society, consult POLANYI, Karl, *The Great Transformation*, Boston: Beacon, 1957 and *Trade and Markets in the Early Empires*, New York: Free Press, 1957. SMELSER, Neil J., 'A Comparative View of Exchange Systems', in: *Economic Development and Cultural Change*, 7, 1959, pp. 173–82, though now dated, remains an excellent introduction to the influence which Polanyi has had. Notice that HUMPHREYS, S. C., 'History, Economics and Anthropology: The Work of Karl Polanyi', in: *History and Theory*, Vol. 8, pp. 165–212, contrary to Polanyi maintains that mastery over scarce means is one of the necessary ingredients in defining the economy in a way which can be compared from society to society. A special issue of *Annales, Economies, Sociétés, Civilisations*, no. 6, Nov.-Dec. 1974, tries to evaluate Polanyi. See: MEILLASSOUX, C., 'Essai d'interprétation du phénomène économique dans les sociétés traditionelles d'auto-subsistence', in: *Cahiers d'Etudes Africaines*, Vol. 1, no. 4, pp. 38–67, for a frustrating attempt to combine Polanyi's understanding with French Marxism.

DUMONT, Louis, *Homo Equalis*, Paris: Gallimard, 1977. (Engl.: *From Mandeville to Marx: Genesis and Triumph of Economic Ideology*, Chicago: Chicago Univ. Press, 1977), is my preferred guide to the ideological redefinition of human nature that happened parallel to the transformation of human desire. Complement with MACPHERSON, C. B., *The Political Theory of Possessive Individualism*, London: Oxford Univ. Press, 1962; and *Democratic Theory*, Oxford: Clarendon Press, 1973. On utilitarianism, HALEVY, Elie, *The Growth of Philosophic Radicalism*, Clifton: Kelley Publ. 1972 (Transl. and abr. from the French).

One of my major problems became the restrictions and qualifications that had to be attached to most terms of formal economics whenever these are used to describe non-monetized social reality. The reality that deals with applicability of formal economic concepts in anthropology can be found in DALTON, G., 'Theoretical Issues in Economic Anthropology', in: *Current Anthropology*, Vol. 10, no. 7, pp. 63–102, 1969. With the critical evaluation of the New Economists who expand economic analysis to the informal sector of contemporary societies, Dupuy will be dealing in a forthcoming book. *My* main concern is the difference in the qualification that must be attached to economic terms, ex. gr., 'scarcity', when this term is applied to describe first the lack of food during a famine among the Barotse, and then to the lack of time of a nervous housewife.

A new look at Unemployment

In a society that aims at full employment, most people who do unpaid work are not counted as 'unemployed'. If "the concept of unemployment was beyond the scope of any idea which early Victorian reformers had at their command, largely because they had no word for it . . . (G. M. YOUNG, Victorian England) or if . . . (Victorians by their avoidance of the term) . . . proved their lack of understanding (of crowd feelings) as E. P. THOMPSON (*Making of the English Working Class*) would claim", consult WILLIAMS, Raymond, *Keywords: A Vocabulary of Culture and Society*, New York: Oxford Univ. Press, 1976, pp. 273–5.

See also GARRATY, John A., *Unemployment in History: Economic Thought and Public Policy*, New York: Harper & Row, 1978. In his introduction the author says: ". . . no one has ever before

written a general history of unemployment . . . I call this book
Unemployment in History instead of a History of Unemployment . . . It does not attempt to describe why there was unemployment, but how the condition of being without work has
been perceived and dealt with in different societies from the
beginning of recorded history . . ." The book exemplifies the
futility of using modern concepts for historical research.

Toward a history of the Household

I argue that the activity, which in ordinary modern language
is called 'housework', must be understood as substantially distinct from that which outside industrial society takes place
within the framework of a 'house'. For the common Indo-
Germanic attitudes towards the house, see BENVENISTE, Emile,
Le vocabulaire des institutions indo-européennes, Vol. 1, Paris: Ed. de
Minuit, 1969, p. 295ff. A synthetic and clear introduction to the
place of the house in old European subsistence in BRUNNER,
Otto, 'Das ganze Haus und die altereuropäische Oekonomie',
in: BRUNNER, Otto, *Neue Wege zur Verfassungs und Sozialgeschichte*,
Göttingen, 1968. FLANDRIN, Jean-Louis, *Familles: parenté, maison,
sexualité dans l'ancienne société*, Paris: Hachette, 1976. RYKWERT,
Joseph, *On Adam's House in Paradise*, New York: Museum of
Modern Art, 1972, and RYKWERT, Joseph, *The Idea of a Town:
The Anthropology of Urban Form in Rome, Italy and the Ancient
World*, Princeton Univ. Press, 1976, are introductions to the
theoretical background of modern architecture. See also: ELIAS,
Norbert, *Die höfische Gesellschaft*, Darmstadt: Luchterhand,
1977. My reading of these leads me to believe that just as health
has been 'medicalized' in contemporary societies, so the perception of space has been professionalized. Modern space is
arranged for a human being as it is perceived by the architect
at the service of his colleagues from the medical, paedagogical
and economic professions.

On the genesis of this essay

After finishing *Medical Nemesis*, I decided to elaborate on the
key chapter of that book: chap. 3 in the draft version, Boyars,
London 1974 and in *Némésis médicale*, Seuil 1975; chap. 6 in

Medical Nemesis as definitively published by Pantheon, New York, 1976, and simultaneously as *Limits to Medicine* by Boyars. Under the guidance of J. P. Dupuy I began to read into the history of economic analysis. I became increasingly fascinated with those aspects of commodity-intensive society that economists tend to relegate to the 'informal sector'; I became interested in them precisely from that point of view under which the economic searchlight envelops them in a deep shadow. The common characteristics of these shadow-transactions I began to call the 'shadow economy'. Phenomenologically this shadow economy revealed characteristics which distinguished it from 'embedded' subsistence activities as well as from formally economic transactions. Having studied for almost a decade the student, the computer, the patient, I found their behavior as actors in the shadow economy, as collaborators in disciplined frustration, thoroughly comparable. To clarify this issue I wrote a paper on *Taught Mother Tongue,* see: *CoEvolution Quart.* Then I came across two papers that oriented my further readings, both, according to their authors, are only 'drafts': WERLHOF, Claudia von, *Frauenarbeit: Der blinde Fleck in der Kritik der politischen Oekonomie*, Bielefeld 1978. (Engl. *Women's Work: The Blindspot in the Critique of Political Economy*.) Both versions are available from: Universität Bielefeld, Soziologische Fakultät. Postfach 8640, 4800 Bielefeld 1.; and BOCK, G. und DUDEN, B., 'Zur Entstehung der Hausarbeit im Kapitalismus', in: *Frauen und Wissenschaft*, Berlin: Courage Verlag, July 1977, pp. 118–99, contains up to 1975 the most stimulating bibliography on the activities typical for enclosed women. The study of these two papers led me to the conviction that the activity for which the modern housewife is the prototype has no parallel outside of industrial society; that this activity is fundamental for the existence of such a society; that contemporary wage labor could come into existence only thanks to the simultaneous structuring of this new kind of activity. I discovered, therefore, in the work that women do in the domestic sphere of a modern economy, the prototype for transactions by students, patients, commuters, and other captive consumers whom I had been studying.

In female housework I began to see the expression of two distinct degradations: an unprecedented degradation of women, and an unprecedented degradation of work, be this kind of work done by women, men, or in-betweens such as children and patients. It seemed to me that the full importance of the unique industrial-age degradation of women will never be adequately understood unless the bifurcation between 'work' and 'shadow work' has first been clearly established. Housework is the key example for shadow work.

If we want to reduce shadow work, we must first clarify what it is. The shady housework of modern women, for instance, is not what women always did. This two French books just published prove by refined indirection: SEGALEN, Martine, *Mari et femme dans la société paysanne*, Paris: Flammarion, 1980, and VERDIER, Yvonne, *Façons de dire, façons de faire: la laveuse, la courturière, la cuisinière*, Paris: Gallimard, 1979. Both express on every page the happy surprise of the authors, modern women, as they reconstruct from the living traces it has left in rural France, the vernacular life of the last century. Housewives are, however, only one category that is currently resisting shadow work. All around the world thousands of movements try to unplug their communities from both wage and shadow work through the choice of an alternative use-value oriented life style. BORREMANS, Valentina, *Reference Guide to Convivial Tools*, New York: The Library Journal, Special Report no. 13. (1180 Avenue of the Americas, New York 10036.) identifies at least 400 reference books to this enormous though almost unnoticed universe, reviewed by Michel BOSQUET, 'L'Archipel de la convivialité', in: *Le Nouvel Observateur*, 31 Dec. 1979, p. 43, ". . . révèlera à des centaines de milliers d'individus qui se croyaient marginaux qu'ils forment en réalité un archipel immense dont, pour la première fois, un livre d'exploration commence de recenser les îles et d'indiquer les contours."

Payment for shadow work

Some forms of work in contemporary society that, at first, seem to be unpaid, are ultimately highly rewarded in monetary terms. University studies are often a good example. The *numerus clausus* obligates a student to embark on a career that he does not like and to acquire competences and notions that are in no provable way related to the performance of his future functions. It is socially inevitable, frustrating and often exacting work. Typically, however, the life-time income of a college graduate will be very much higher than of his non-graduate brothers and sisters. His non-monetary perquisites will also be much higher. Pro-rating this extra income per hour of cramming for exams in a school of accounting makes these hours into some of the best paid in society. Unlike the first twelve years of schooling that are made obligatory by life-long social sanctions against the dropout, 'work' done in college could be considered part of a well paid life-time job. The fact that everywhere in the world university students organize for higher scholarships can perhaps be interpreted as evidence for the fact that they do feel themselves already as 'workers'.

This is obviously not so for authentic shadow workers: full-time housewives, middle-school pupils, part-time commuters. Their claim to compensation is of a different kind. When they succeed to transform an activity that, in 1970, was exacted as unpaid shadow work into paid labor by 1980, they have re-defined their type of activity. In Sweden, for instance, some housewives are now paid wages, and some factory workers have negotiated through their unions a bonus for each hour spent commuting to the job. Their employers recognize that their workday begins when they leave their homes.

I am therefore not arguing that some unpaid work, now performed in view of a future recompense, could not be paid in advance; nor am I arguing that some shadow work cannot be transformed into wage labor. What I argue is something else: the creation of new wage labor inevitably also generates new shadow work. New social services inevitably increase the disciplined acquiescence of clients. What is worse: shadow workers can be used to create shadow work of others. In fact, Sweden might now be leading the world in the attempt to employ disciplined shadow workers (volunteers) in its social services. See: 'Working Life in the Future – Programme for a Future Study', and 'Care in Society – A Project Presentation', published by the Secretariat for Future Studies, Box 7502, S-103 92 Stockholm. This is a plan to make shadow work in the social sector increase much faster than wage labor. Philanthropy was used in this way since the evangelical campaigns in England in the 1810s.

To page 100

Subsistence

Should I use the term? Until a few years ago in English it was monopolized by 'subsistence agriculture'; this meant billions living on 'bare survival', the lot from which development agencies were to save them. Or it meant the lowest level to which a bum could sink on skid-row. Or, finally, it was identified with wages. To avoid these confusions, in the essay *The Three Dimensions of Public Choice* (pp. 9–26), I have proposed the use of the term 'vernacular'. This is a technical term used by Roman lawyers for the inverse of a commodity. 'Vernaculum, Quidquid domi nascitur, domestici fructus, res, quae alicui nata est, et quam non emit. Ita hanc vocem interpretatur Anianus in leg. 3. Cod. Th. de lustrali collatione, ubi Jacob. Gothofredus." Du Cange, *Glossarium Mediae et Infimae Latinitatis*, Vol. VIII, p. 283.

I want to speak about vernacular activity and vernacular domain. Nevertheless, here, I am avoiding these expressions because I cannot expect my readers of this essay alone to be acquainted with 'Vernacular Values' (but see Part I of this book). Use-value oriented activities, non-monetary transactions, embedded economic activities, substantive economics, these all are terms which have been tried. I stick to 'subsistence' in this paper. I will oppose subsistence-oriented activities to those which are at the service of a formal economy, no matter if these economic activities are paid or not. And, within the realm of economic activities, I will distinguish a formal and an informal sector, to which wage and shadow work correspond.

Sachs, Ignacy et Schiray, M., *Styles de vie et de développement dans le monde occidental: expériences et expérimentations*. Regional Seminar on Alternative Patterns of Development and Life Styles for the African Region, December 1978. Cired, 54 Boul. Raspail, Paris 6., attempts a similar distinction between true and phoney use-values: "... le hors-marché recouvre deux réalités fort différentes, les prestations de services gratuits par l'Etat et la production autonome de valeurs d'usage ... Les pseudo-valeurs d'usage n'apportent aucune satisfaction positive de besoin autre que la satisfaction de posséder plus." For background on this: Sachs, Ignacy, "La notion du surplus et son application aux économies primitives', in: *L'Homme*, Vol. VI, no. 3, July–Sept. 1966, pp. 5–18; and EGNER, Erich, *Hauswirtschaft und Lebenshaltung*, Berlin: Duncker & Humbolt, 1974. An interesting international seminar on subsistence has been held at Bielefeld University, Soziologische Fakultät.

To page 101

The semantic of work

On the comparative semantics of the key-word 'work' in the main languages of Europe, consult: KNOBLOCH, J. et al., *Europaeische Schluesselwoerter*, Vol. II. *Kurzmonographien*, Muenchen: Max Hueber, 1964, especially the contributions by KRUPP, Meta. 'Wortfeld "Arbeit" ', pp. 258–6; GRAACH, Harmut, 'Labor and Work', pp. 287–316; and MEURERS, Walter, 'Job', pp. 317–54. R. Williams, op cit. in a few pages, 282ff., describes vividly the shift of 'work' from the productive effort of individual people to the predominant social relationship. For a broad, well-documented study, consult: BRUNNER, O.; CONZE, W.; und KOSELLECK, R., eds. *Geschichtliche Grundbegriffe*, the articles by Werner CONZE, on 'Arbeit' and 'Arbeiter', Vol. 1, pp. 154–243. This monumental Lexikon (subtitled Historisches Lexikon zur Politisch-sozialen Sprache in Deutschland) will be completed in the late 1980s in 7 volumes. About 130 keywords that have undergone a major semantic change with the coming of industrial society, have been selected. On each term, the history of its political and social use is given. Though each monograph focuses on the use of a German term, the bibliography mentions important parallel studies for other European languages. Though dated, an excellent guide to the historical semantics of socialist terminology, mainly concerned with work is BESTOR, Arthur E. Jr., 'The Evolution of the Socialist Vocabulary', in: *Journal of the History of Ideas*, Vol. 9, no. 3, June 1948, pp. 259–302. See also FEBVRE, Lucien, 'Travail, évolution d'un mot et d'une idée', in: *Journal de Psychologie normale et pathologique*, Vol. 41, no. 1, 1948, pp. 19–28; and TOURAINE, A., 'La quantification du travail: histoire d'une notion', in: *Le Travail, les Métiers, l'Emploi*, special number of *Journal de Psychologie*, 1955, pp. 97–112. For the Middle Ages:

WILPERT, Paul, ed. *Beitraege zum Berufsbewusstsein des mittelalter-lichen Menschen*, Miscelanea Medievalis, Vol. III, Berlin 1964; DELARUELLE, Etienne, 'Le travail dans les règles monastiques occidentales du IV° au IX° siècles', in: *Journal de Psychologie normale et pathologique*, Vol. XVI, no. 1, 1948, pp. 51–62; STAHLEDER, Helmuth, *Arbeit in der mittelalterlichen Gesellschaft*, Muenchen: Neue Schriftenreihe des Stadtarchivs Muenchen, 1972. For the relationship between the meaning of work and technology in the Middle Ages: WHITE, Lynn, Jr., 'Medieval Engineering and the Sociology of Knowledge', in: *Pacific Historical Review*, no. 44, 1975, pp. 1–21. The impact of Luther on the meaning of work is well dealt with in GEIST, Hildburg, 'Arbeit: die Entscheidung eines Wortwertes durch Luther', in: *Luther Jahrbuch*, 1931, pp. 83–113. Notice MENCKEN, H. L., *A Mencken Chrestomancy*, New York 1953, p. 107: "It remains for the heretic Martin Luther to discover that the thing was laudable in itself. He was the true inventor of the modern doctrine that there is something inherently dignified and praiseworthy about labor, that the man who bears the burden in the heart of the day is somehow more pleasing to God than the man who takes his ease in the shade." For the nineteenth century see also AMBROS, D. und SPECHT, K. G., 'Zur Ideologisierung der Arbeit', in: *Studium Generale*, Heft 4, 14.Jahrgang, 1961, pp. 199–207.

The linguistic colonization

See LECLERC, J., 'Vocabulaire social et répression politique: un exemple indonésien', in: *Annales ESC.*, no. 28, 1973, pp. 407–82. For background consult also ANDERSON, Ben, 'The language of Indonesian Politics', in: *Indonesia*, Cornell Univ., April 1966, pp. 89–116; and HINLOOPEN-LABBERTON, D. van, *Dictionnaire de termes de droit coutumier indonésien*, Nijhof, Den Haag, 1934. See also ILLICH, Ivan, 'El derecho al desempleo creador', in: *Tecno-Politica*, Doc. 78/11, Cuernavaca.

Servile work and Hannah Arendt

ARENDT, Hannah, *The Human Condition*, New York: Anchor Book, 1959, has beautiful chapters on labor and work that are frequently referred to. They are valuable insofar as they sum up a Western, civilized consensus on a distinction between the reign of necessity and that of freedom, a distinction that was repeated frequently from Plato to Marx. But the unexamined acceptance of Arendt's philosophical interpretation as an history of work tends to veil the discontinuity in the status of work during the transition to industrial society. I argue that in the classical sense of Hannah Arendt, the social conditions for both labor and work have been destroyed. On servile work, see also: VERNANT, J. P., 'Travail et nature dans la Grèce ancienne', in: *Journal de Psychologie normale et pathologique*, Vol. 52, no. 1, 1955, pp. 18–38; NEURATH, Otto, 'Beitraege zur Geschichte der Opera Servilia', in: *Archiv fuer Sozialwissenschaften und Sozialpolitik*, Vol. 51, no. 2, 1915, pp. 438–65; and BRAUN, Pierre, 'Le tabou des Feriae', in: *L'Année sociologique*, 3rd series, 1959, pp. 49–125.

To page 102

Work and the Church

The place of work as a keyword in Catholic thinking can be gauged from the following observations: the single most encyclopedic reference on Catholicism is the 25 volume *Dictionnaire de Théologie Catholique*. When, after forty years of publication, the last but one fascicule of the index was published in 1971, the editors added in the midst of the subject index a 6000-word essay to 'travail' which begins with the sentence: "the absence of such an article in this encyclopedia is the symptom of a lacuna in theology . . .". I intend to prepare a study guide to the contribution of the major churches in the nineteenth century to the evolution of shadow work – mainly under the form of social and housework – and to the parallel evolution of a 'Christian' ideology that ascribes dignity to wage labor.

The best guide to bibliography seems to be the series of articles on "Arbeit" in: *Theologische Realenzyklopädie*. On the violence done in the name of gender by American disestablished religion during the mid-nineteenth century, I was impressed by the analysis made by DOUGLAS, Ann, *The Feminization of American Culture*, New York: Avon Books, 1978.

See also HALL, Catherine, 'The Early Formation of Victorian Domestic Ideology', in: BURMAN, S., *Fit Work for Women*, London: Croom Helm, 1979, pp. 15–32. As productive work moved from the home to the factory, evangelical campaigns (1780–1820), parallel to Wesley's Methodism in the U.S., led to the consolidation of a domestic sphere in which women did their *duties* while men went out to *work*. Women not working became the only proper way for them to live. As Elie HALEVY, op. cit., first noticed, in the late eighteenth century the religious became linked with the domestic and thus the private world of morality could be opposed to the a-moral, a-theological world of economics.

SCHUMPETER, Joseph A., *History of Economic Analysis*, London: Allen & Unwin, 1954, p. 270: "In principle, medieval society provided a berth for everyone whom it recognized as a member: its structural design excluded unemployment and destitution".

HOBSBAWN, E. J., 'Poverty', in: *Encyclopedia of Social Science*. Pauperism arose historically beyond the border of the functioning primary social group . . . a man's wife and children were not ipso facto paupers, but widows and orphans, who stood in danger of losing their berth were perhaps the earliest clearly-defined category of persons with a call upon public assistance.

Medieval attitudes towards poverty and towards work

The attitude that people had towards the weak, hungry, sick, homeless, landless, mad, imprisoned, enslaved, fugitive, orphaned, exiled, crippled, beggars, ascetics, streetvendors, soldiers, foundlings and others who were relatively deprived has changed throughout history. For every epoch, specific attitudes to each of these categories are in a unique constellation. Economic history, when it studies poverty, tends to neglect these attitudes. Economic history tends to focus on measurements of average and median calory intake, group-specific mortality rates, the polarisation in the use of resources, etc. . . .

During the last decade, the historical study of attitudes toward poverty has made considerable progress. For late antiquity and the Middle Ages, see: MOLLAT, Michel, *Etudes sur l'histoire de la pauvreté*, Série 'Etudes', Vol. 8, Publications de la Sorbonne, Paris, collects a selection of three dozen studies submitted to his seminar. POLICA, Gabriella Severina, 'Storia della poverta e storia dei poveri', in: *Studi Medievali*, Vol. 17, 1976, pp. 363–91, surveys the recent literature. On the cyclical experience of poverty in the Middle Ages, see: DUBY, Georges, "Les pauvres des campagnes dans l'Occident médiéval jusqu'au XIII° siècle', in: *Revue d'Histoire de l'Eglise de France*, Vol. 52, 1966, pp. 25–33. Some of the most valuable contributions have been made by a Polish historian: GEREMEK, Bronislav, 'Criminalité, vagabondage, pauperisme: la marginalité à l'aube des temps modernes', in: *Revue d'Histoire moderne et contemporaine*, Vol. 21, 1974, pp. 337–75, and, by the same author, *Les marginaux parisiens aux XIV° et XV° siècles*, Paris: Flammarion, 1976. Translated from the Russian, a delightful book is BAKHTINE, Mikkaïl, *Rabelais and his World*, Transl. by Hélène Iswolsky, M.I.T. Press, 1971. In French: *L'oeuvre de François Rabelais et la culture populaire au Moyen Age et sous la Renaissance*, transl. by Andrée Robel, Gallimard, 1970. He describes how the poor projected their self-image in carnivals, festivals, farces.

GEREMEK, B., *Le salariat dans l'artisanat parisien au XII° siècle*, Paris, Mouton, 1968, indicates clearly that legitimate wage earners were only those who derived most of their subsistence from participation in the household of their employers. See also STAHLEDER, Helmuth, op. cit.

The non-economic perception of poverty

The comparative study of attitudes toward poverty in the Eastern and the Western Middle Ages sheds light on this point. PATLAGEAN, Evelyne, 'La pauvreté à Byzance au temps de Justinien: les origines d'un modèle politique', in: MOLLAT, M., op. cit., Vol. 1, pp. 59–81, argues that in urbanized Byzantium the law recognized poverty as a primarily economic condition long before such recognition became possible in continental Europe.

BOSL, Karl, ' "Potens" und "Pauper": Begriffsgeschichtliche Studien zur Gesellschaftlichen Differenzierung im fruehen

Mittelalter und zum Pauperismus des Hochmittelalters', in: *Festschrift O. Brunner*, Göttingen, 1963, pp. 601–87.

To page 103

LADNER, G., 'Homo Viator: medieval Ideas on Alienation and Order', in: *Speculum*, Vol. 42, 1967, pp. 233–59, masterfully describes this attitude: the pilgrim, homo viator, placed between 'ordo' and 'abalienatio' was a fundamental ideal for the Middle Ages. CONVENGNI DEL CENTRO DI STUDI SULLA SPIRITUALITA MEDIEVALE, Vol. III, *Poverta e richezza nella spiritualitá del secolo XI° e XII°*, Italia, Todi, 1969, gathers a dozen contributions about the attitudes toward 'poverty' which complete the collection of Michel Mollat.

COUVREUR, G., *Les pauvres ont-ils des droits? Récherches sur le vol en cas d'extrème nécessité depuis la 'Concordia' de Gratien, 1140, jusqu'á Guillaume d'Auxerre, mort en 1231*, Rome–Paris: Thèse, 1961, is a full study of the legal recognition of rights that derive from poverty during the High Middle Ages. On the legal, canonical expressions given to these rights, consult: TIERNEY, B., *Medieval Poor Law: A Sketch of Canonical Theory and its Applications in England*, Berkeley: Univ. of California Press, 1959.

On Ratger see: ADAM, August, *Arbeit und Besitz nach Ratherus von Verona*, Freiburg, 1927.

To page 104

Enclosure is one way of describing the process by which a popular culture is deprived of its means for subsistence. See POLANYI, Karl, *The Great Transformation*, Boston, Beacon Paperback, 1957, especially chap. 7 'Speenhamland 1795' and chap. 8 'Antecedences and Consequences', pp. 77–102. A particularly sensitive monograph on the process by which the poor were transformed, I found in GUITTON, Jean Pierre, *La société et les pauvres: l'example de la généralité de Lyon, 1534–1789*. Bibliothèque de la Faculté des Lettres, Lyon. No. 26, 1971, ". . . la société au XVIII° siècle, pour reconnaître sa responsbilité dans le paupérisme, condamne à l'extinction les mendiants et les vagabonds comme 'ordre' social. . . . la société marginalise le fond médiéval qui faisait de la pauvreté un signe d'élection, et de l'aumone, . . . le signe de la soldairité organisée."

HALEVY, Elie, op. cit. described the attitude towards the poor as this is reflected in those who write about them in England. In England, ever since the time when the advent of protestantism had brought about the disappearance of the monasteries, the law had recognized the right of the indigent, the infirm, the beggars, but also the laborers whose wages did not keep them from want to assistance offered by the nation. The right to sustenance was written into the law in 1562, 1572 and 1601. In every parish, Justices of the Peace were empowered to levy a poor rate on the inhabitants. Only in the early eighteenth century, the tax-payers began to protest effectively against this imposition, and by 1722, the workhouse received the seal of the law. The newer formula of the right to work superseded the traditional guaranteed right to existence.

Reports on the destruction of European popular culture

The modern age can be understood as that of an unrelenting 500-year war waged to destroy the environmental conditions for subsistence and to replace them by commodities produced within the frame of the new nation state. In this war against popular cultures and their framework, the State was at first assisted by the clergies of the various churches, and later by the professionals and their institutional procedures. During this war, popular cultures and vernacular domains – areas of subsistence – were devastated on all levels. Modern history, from the point of view of the losers in this war, still remains to be written. The report on this war has so far reflected the belief that it helped 'the poor' toward progress. It was written from the point of view of the winners. Marxist historians are usually not less blinded to the values that were destroyed than their bourgeois, liberal or Christian colleagues. Economic historians tend to start their research with categories that reflect the foregone conclusion that scarcity, defined by mimetic desire, is the human condition par excellence.

The single most encouraging exception to this historiographic tradition is a group of French historians formed mostly around

and by the journal *Les Annales, Economies, Sociétés, Civilisations,*
Editorial Office: 54 Boulevard Raspail, Paris 6. Subscriptions:
Libraririe Armand Colin, 103 Boulevard Saint Michel, Paris 5.
For more than a generation they have refined and tested methods
and hypotheses that make the historical study of popular subsistence cultures feasible. They have hunted for documents that
preserve the actual words of the illiterate which they could use
to interpret the few archeological remains of the poor that have
not rotted away. On gravestones and in songs, in streetsellers'
cries, in farce and riddles, and above all in the testimonies taken
down by courts from rogues, adulterers and witches, they have
found the faint traces of the mentality, the sensibility, the
mythology of that majority in every past age that has usually
been illiterate, which concretely means: deprived of the services
of a scribe.

For a reading of modern history as a war on subsistence, my
preferred introduction is MUCHEMBLED, Robert, *Culture populaire
et culture des élites dans la France moderne du XV° au XVIII° siecles,*
Paris: Flammarion, 1978, which can fruitfully be comple-
mented by CASTAN, Y., *Honnèteté et relations sociales en Languedoc,
1715–1780,* Paris: Plon, 1974. LE ROY LADURIE, Emmanuel,
Montaillou, village occitan de 1294 à 1324, Paris: Gallimard, 1975,
shows how a master can reconstruct the life of a medieval
village. I strongly recommend the reading of DELUMEAU, Jean,
La peur en Occident, XIV°–XVII° siècles, Paris: Fayard, 1978. It
is a major history of the experience of fear, and the various forms
that fear has taken in, and since, the Middle Ages. Inevitably,
contemporaries are frightened by the idea that survival could
be based on subsistence. This personal fear might be one of the
major obstacles because of which contemporaries are almost
incapable of considering a world in which an alternative use of
technology would put modern forms of subsistence at the center
of public concern. With fear, attitudes towards death and child-
hood have also profoundly changed. ARIES, Philippe, *L'homme
devant la mort,* Paris: Seuil, 1977; and *L'enfant et la vie familiale
sous l'ancien régime,* Paris: Plon, 1960. GINZBURG, C., *Il formaggio
e i vermi,* Turin: Einaudi Paperbacks 65, 1976, introduces to
Italian studies on the organization of local subsistence and its
destruction. On the 'sacrifice du patois sur l'autel de la patrie',
see CERTEAU, Michel de.

ADAMS, Thomas M., 'Mendicity and Moral Alchemy: Work as Rehabilitation', in: *Studies on Voltaire and the XVIII° century*, Vol. 151, 1976.

What Bertrand RUSSEL said in *Praise of Ideleness*, London: George Allen, 1960, about landowners (p. 17) can just as well be said about the learned. ". . . the gospel of work which has led the rich . . . to preach the dignity of labor, while taking care themselves to remain undignified in this respect."

FERBER, Christian von, *Arbeitsfreude: Wirklichkeit und die Ideologie. Ein Beitrag zur Soziologie der Arbeit in der industriellen Gesellschaft*, Stuttgart: Enke, 1959.

To page 105

The metaphors Marx uses all the time are far from being simple metaphors: the Substance Labor is cristalized in products; it is deposited, congealed in them; it exists as an amorphous gelatine, it is decanted from one product into another. Engels exposes explicit the dialectic of chemistry but, page after page, the alchemistry comes through that 'reduces' the social historical into physiology, and vice versa. For Marx, the epiphany of value lies in the materialization of the faculties that are originally sleeping in man, and awaken only through his transformation into an industrial producer. CASTORIADIS, Cornelius, "From Marx to Aristotle, from Aristotle to us", in: *Social Research*, Vol. 45, no. 84, 1978, pp. 667–738 (translated from the French by Andrew Arato), pp. 672 ff.

HEILBRONER, R. L., *Business Civilization in Decline*, New York: Norton; London: Marion Boyars.

HUFTON, O., *The Poor in XVIII° century France*, Oxford: Clarendon Press, 1974.

TAWNEY, R. H., *Religion and the Rise of Capitalism*, 1926, pp. 254 ff argues that in England a hardening of the attitude toward the poor can be noticed in the late seventeenth century when poverty is first identified with vice. MARSHALL, Dorothy, *The*

English Poor in the XVIII° Century: A Study in Social and Administrative History, London: 1926, p. 20., finds this hardening of attitudes only at the beginning of the eighteenth century, but not earlier than R. H. Tawney. See also: MARSHALL, Dorothy, 'The Old Poor Law, 1662–1795', in: CARUS-WILSON, E. M., *Essays in Economic History*, Vol. 1, pp. 295–305.

GEREMEK, B., 'Renfermement des pauvres en Italie, XIV–XVII° siècles', in: *Mélanges en l'honneur de F. Braudel*, I, Toulouse 1973.

To page 106

KRUEGER, Horst, *Zur Geschichte der Manufakturen und Manufakturarbeiter in Preussen*, Berlin, DBR: Ruetten und Loening, 1958, p. 598.

Moral Economy

On the proto-industrial crowd: THOMPSON, Edward P., *The Making of the English Working Class*, New York, Random House, 1966, has become a classic. BREWER, John, and STYLES, John, *An Ungovernable People: the English and their Law in the XVII° and XVIII° centuries*, Rutgers Univ. Press, 1979, gather materials for the first major factual critique of Thompson. In England, at least, criminal rather than civil law was used by the élite to repress the crowd. Thompson's basic insight about the existence of a moral economy is confirmed by the new study. See also MEDICK, Hans, 'The proto-industrial Family Economy: the Structural Functions of Household and Family during the transition from Peasant Society to Industrial Capitalism', in: *Social History*, 1, 1976, pp. 291–315, so far the clearest statement on this transition that I have seen. Complement this, especially for a new bibliography, with MEDICK, Hans and SABEAN, David, 'Family and Kinship: Material Interest and Emotion', in: *Peasant Studies*, Vol. 8, no. 2, 1979, pp. 139–60.

Four issues on the division of labor that must not be confused

These four issues are intimately related, but cannot be clarified unless they are separately discussed.

1. It becomes increasingly obvious that there is no proven correlation between education for a specialized function and the technical competence for the performance of this function. Further, the basic assumptions on which a socialist critique of a capitalist division of labor were built have ceased to hold. See the introduction to GORZ, André, *Critique de la division du travail*, Paris: Seuil, 1973. In German: 'Kritik der Arbeitsteilung', in: *Technologie und Politik*, n° 8, pp. 137–47; and GORZ, André, *Adieux au prolétariat: au delà du socialism*, Paris: Galilée, 1980. "Les forces productives dévelopées par le capitalisme en portent à tel point l'empreinte, qu'elles ne peuvent être gérées ni mises en oeuvre selon une rationalité socialiste... Le capitalisme a fait naitre une classe ouvrière dont les intérêts, les capacités, les qualifications, sont fonction de forces productives, elles-mêmes fonctionnelles par rapport à la seule rationalité capitaliste. Le dépassement du capitalisme ... ne peut dès lors provenir que de couches qui représentent ou préfigurent la dissolution de toutes les classes, y compris de la classe ouvrière elle-même ... La division capitaliste du travail a détruit le double fondement du 'socialisme scientifique' – le travail ouvrier ne comporte plus de pouvoir et il n'est plus une activité propre du travailleur. L'ouvrier traditionnel n'est plus qu'une minorité privilégiée. La majorité de la population appartient à ce néo-prolétariat post-industriel des sans-statut et des sans-classe ... surqualifiés. ... Ils ne peuvent se reconnaitre dans l'appelation de 'travailleur', ni dans celle, symétrique, de 'chomeur' ... la société produit pour faire du travail ... le travail devient astreinte inutile pour laquelle la société cherche à masquer aux individus leur chomage ... le travailleur assiste à son devenir comme à un processus étranger et à un spectacle.'

2. A new trend in the history of technology is represented by KUBY, Thomas, 'Ueber den Gesellschaftlichen Ursprung der Maschine', in: *Technologie und Politik*, n° 16, 1980, pp. 71–103 (English version in forthcoming *The Convivial Archipelago*, edited by Valentina BORREMANS, 1981). Summary of a forth-coming important study on Sir Richard Arkwright, the barber and wigmaker who in 1767 constructed the first spinning machine that could make cotton yarn suitable for warps. His invention is usually seen as a linear progress beyond Hargrave's spinning jenny – at that time already power-driven – that could

make yarn only for weft. Division of labor was not a necessary implication of technical improvement needed to increase production. Rather, increased productivity could not be exacted from workers without organizing technical processes in such manner that they also reduced workers to disciplined cogs attached to a machine. For a splendid introduciton to the history of thought on the relationship between freedom and techniques see ULRICH, Otto, *Technik und Herrschaft*, Frankfurt: Suhrkamp, 1977. Also MARGLIN, Stephen, 'What do bosses do?', in: *Review of Radical Political Economics*, VI, Summer 1974, pp. 60–112; VII, Spring 1975, pp. 20–37, argues that the nineteenth century factory system developed not due to a technological superiority over handicraft production, but due to its more effective control of the labor force that it gave to the employer.

3. A third aspect under which the division of labor is currently discussed is the culture-specific assignment of tasks between the sexes. See next note.

4. The economic division of labor into a productive and a non-productive kind is a fourth issue which must not be confused with any of the first three. BAULANT, M., 'La famille en miettes', in: *Annales*, no. X, 1972, p. 960ff. For the process see MEDICK, Hans, op. cit. previous note. It is the economic redefinition of sexes in the nineteenth century. I will show that this 'sexual' character has been veiled in the nineteenth century.

To page 107

Division of labor by sex

No two non-industrial societies assign tasks to men and to women in the same way, MEAD, Margaret, *Male and Female: A Study of the Sexes in a Changing World*, New York: Dell Publ., 1968, especially pp. 178ff. Clear, to the point, and with good bibliography are: ROBERTS, Michael, 'Sickles and Scythes: Women's Work and Men's Work at Harvest Time', in: *History Workshop*, 7, 1979, pp. 3–28, and BROWN, Judith, 'A Note on the Division of Labor by Sex', in: *American Anthropologist*, 72, 1970, pp. 1073–8. For illustrations from the recent English past see: KITTERINGHAM, Jennie, 'Country Work Girls in XIX°

century England', in: SAMUEL, Raphael, ed., *Village Life and Labor*, London–Boston: Routledge and Kegan Paul, 1975, pp. 73–138. A survey: WHITE, Martin K., *The Status of Women in Pre-Industrial Societies*, Princeton Univ. Press, 1976. For bibliography, consult MILDEN, James, *The Family in Past Time: A Guide to Literature*, Garland, 1977; and ROGERS, S. C., 'Woman's Place: A Critical Review of Anthropological Theory', in: *Comparative Studies of Society and History*, 20, 1978, pp. 123–67. This cultural division of labor by sex must not be confused with the economic division of labor into the primarily productive man and the primarily, or naturally, reproductive woman, that came into being during the nineteenth century.

The modern couple and the nuclear family

The nuclear family is not new. What is without precedent is a society which elevates the subsistence-less family into the norm and thereby discriminates against all types of bonds between two people that do not take their model from this new family.

The new entity came into being as the wage earner's family in the nineteneth century. Its purpose was that of coupling one principal wage earner and his shadow. The household became the place where the consumption of wages takes place. HAUSEN, Karin, 'Die Polarisierung des Geschlechtscharakters: eine Spiegelung der Dissoziation von Erwerbs und Familienleben', in: *Sozialgeschichte der Familie in der Neuzeit Europas, Neue Forschung*. Edited by W. CONZE, Stuttgart, 1976, pp. 367–93. This remains true even today when in many cases all members of a household are both wage earners and active homebodies. It remains true even for the 'single's' home equipped with 'one-person-household-ice-box'.

This new economic function of the family is often veiled by discussion about 'nuclear family'. Nuclear family, conjugally organized households, can exist and have existed throughout history as the norm in societies in which the coupling of subsistence-less people would not have been conceivable. VEYNE, Paul, 'La famille et l'amour sous le Haut-Empire romain', in: *Annales*, 33rd year, no. 1, Jan.–Feb. 1978, pp. 35–63, claims that between Augustus and the Antonines in Rome, independently from any Christian influence, the ideal of a nuclear, conjugal family had come into being. It was in the interest of the owners to make this kind of family obligatory for their slaves. In its aristocratic form, it was taken over by Christians. DUBY, Georges, *La société aux XI° et XII° siècles dans la région maconnaise*, Paris 1953, and HERLIHY, David, 'Family Solidarity in Medieval Italian History', in: *Economy, Society and Government in Medieval Italy*, Kent State Univ. Press, 1969, pp. 173–9, see the early European family typically reduced to a conjugal cell into well into the twelfth century. Then, a process of consolidation begins that is concerned mainly with land-holdings. Canon law has little influence on it. See also PELLE-GRINI, Giovan Battista, 'Terminologia matrimoniale', in: *Settimane di Studio del Centro Italiano per l'Alto Medioevo di Spoleto*, 1977, pp. 43–102, which introduces the complex terminology, or set of terminologies, which are necessary to understand medieval marriage. See also METRAL, M. O., *Le mariage: les hésitations de l'Occident*. Foreword by Philippe Ariès, Paris: Aubier, 1977. For the seventeenth and eighteenth centuries I found useful ARIES, Philippe, *L'enfant et la vie familiale sous l'ancien régime*, Plon, 1960, and LEBRUN, Francois, *La vie conjugale sous l'ancien régime*, Paris: Colin, 1975. LASLETT, Peter, *Un monde que nous avons perdu: les structures sociales pré-industrielles*, Flammarion, 1969. Engl.: *The World we have lost*, find conjugal families typical for England much before the industrial revolu-tion. BERKNER and SHORTER, Edward. 'La vie intime': Beitraege zur Geschichte am Beispiel des kulturellen Wandels in der Bayrischen Unterschichte im 19. Jh.', in: *Koelner Zeitschrift fuer Soziologie und Sozialpsychologie*, special number 16, 1972, find nuclear families typical for South-Germanic peasants at a certain stage in the life-cycle when the old have died off. It seems probable that the extended family is primarily 'the nostalgia of modern sociologists'.

What makes the modern family unique is the 'social' sphere in which it exists. The O.E.D. gives among nine meanings the third as: "group of persons consisting of the parents and their children, whether actually living together or not", as a meaning that appears in the nineteenth century. Family quarrels, 1801; family life, 1845; unfit for family reading, 1853; family tickets for admission for half the price, 1859; family magazine, 1874.

HERLIHY, David, 'Land, Family and Women in Continental

Europe, 701–1200', in: *Traditio*, 18, 1962, pp. 89–120 (Fordham Univ. N.Y.).

The family as an institution of 'police'

In the subsistent family, the members were tied together by the need of creating their livelihood. In the modern couple-centered family, the members are kept together for the sake of an economy to which they, themselves, are marginal. DONZELOT, Jacques, *La police des familles*, Paris: Ed. de Minuit, 1977. Engl.: *The Policing of Families*, transl. by Robert Hurley, New York: Pantheon, 1979, follows and elaborates FOUCAULD, Michel, *La volonté de savoir*, Paris: Gallimard, 1976, by describing this as 'policing' by which the so-called social domain is created . . . the domain to which we refer when we speak of 'social' work, 'social' scourge, 'social' programs, 'social' advancement. According to J. Donzelot, the history of this domain, and the process by which it comes into being, namely 'policing', can neither be identified with traditional political history, nor with the history of popular culture. It represents a bio-political dimension that uses political techniques to invest the body, health, modes of living and housing, through activities which all were, originally, called policing. Donzelot's attempt to describe the formation of the 'social sphere' will be better understood after reading DUMONT, Louis, 'The Modern Conception of the Individual: Notes on its Genesis and that of Concomitant Institutions', in: *Contributions to Indian Sociology*, no. VIII, October 1965; also Microfiches, Presses de la Fondation des Sciences Politiques. The French translation: "La conception moderne de l'individu: notes sur sa genèse en relation avec les conceptions de la politique et de l'Etat à partir du XIIIe siècle", in: *Esprit*, February, 1978. Louis Dumont describes the simultaneous appearance of the political and the economic sphere. See also Paul Dumouchel's, op. cit. comments on Louis Dumont.

The diagnosis of 'woman'

C. LASCH (*New York Review of Books*, Nov. 24, 1977, p. 16). Recent studies of 'profesionalization' by historians have shown that professionalism did not emerge in the nineteenth century in response to clearly defined social needs. Instead, the new professions themselves invented many of the needs they claimed to satisfy. They played on public fears of disorder and disease, adopted a deliberately mystifying jargon, ridiculed popular traditions and self-help as backward and unscientific. And, in this way, created or intensified – not without opposition – a rising demand for their services. An excellent introduction to this process, with good bibliography, is BLEDSTEIN, Burton J., *The Culture of Professionalism*, New York: Norton, 1976. EHRENREICH, Barbara and ENGLISH, Deirdre, *For Her Own Good: 150 Years of the Expert's Advice to Women*, New York: Anchor, 1978, give the history of the professional control over women. Page 127: "The manufacture of housework . . . after mid-century . . . with less and less to make in the home, it seemed as if there would soon be nothing to do in the home. Educators, popular writers and leading social scientists fretted about the growing void in the home, that Veblen defined as the evidence of wasted efforts . . . i.e. conspicuous consumption. . . . Clergymen and physicians were particularly convincing in their effort to provide their services so as to make 'home life the highest and finest product of civilization' ". On the medicalization of female nature, I found particularly useful: BARKER-BENFIELD, G. J., *The Horrors of the Half-Known Life: Male Attitudes toward Women and Sexuality in the XIX°-Century America*. New York: Harper and Row, 1976; ROSENBERG, Rosalind, 'In search of Woman's Nature: 1850–1920', in: *Feminist Studies*, 3, 1975; SMITH-ROSENBERG, Carroll, 'The Histerical Woman: Sex-roles in XIX° Century America', in: *Social Research*, 39, 1972, pp. 652–78; MCLAREN, Angus, 'Doctor in the House: Medicine and Private Morality in France, 1800–1850', in: *Feminist Studies*, 2, 1975, pp. 39–54; HALLER, John and HALLER, Robin, *The Physician and Sexuality in Victorian America*, Urbana, Ill.: Univ. of Illinois Press, 1974; VICINUS, Marta, *Suffer and be Still: Women in the Victorian Age*, Bloomington: Indiana Univ. Press, 1972; LEACH, E. R., *Culture and Nature or 'La femme sauvage'*, The Stevenson Lecture, November 1968, Bedford College, The University of London; KNIBIEHLER, Y., 'Les médecins et la "nature féminine" au temps du Code Civil', in: *Annales*, 31st year, 4, July–August, 1976, pp. 824–45.

DUDEN, Barbara, 'Das schoene Eigentum', in: *Kursbuch*, 49, 1977, a commentary on Kant's writings on women.

From Mistress to Housewife

See op. cit. BOCK und DUDEN, 'Zur Entstehung der Hausarbeit im Kapitalismus'. DAVIS, Natalie Z., *Society and Culture in Early Modern France*, Stanford Univ. Press, might be a good starting point for somebody unacquainted with the issue, or CONZE, Werner, *Sozialgeschichte der Familie in der Neuzeit Europas*, Stuttgart, 1976. DAVIS, Natalie Z. and CONWAY, Jill K., *Society and the Sexes: A Bibliography of Women's History in Early Modern Europe, Colonial America and the United States*, Garland, 1976, is an indispensable working tool. As a complement, I found useful ROE, Jill, 'Modernization and Sexism: Recent Writings on Victorian Women', in: *Victorian Studies*, 20, 1976–77, pp. 179–92, and MUCHEMBLED, Robert, 'Famille et histoire des mentalités, XVI°–XVIII° siècles: état présent des recherches', in: *Revue des Etudes Sud-Est Européen* (Bucarest), XII, 3, 1974, pp. 349–69, and ROWBOTHAM, Sheila, *Hidden from History: Rediscovering Women in History from the XVII° Century to the Present*, New York: Vintage Books, 1976. The un-numbered page following p. 175 of this second edition, contains a valuable selected bibliography on the change of women's roles in Britain during the early Victorian period. The following two articles question to which degree the traditional periodization, categorization and theories of social change can be applied to recent women's history: BRANCA, Patricia, 'A New Perspective of Women's Work: A Comparative Typology', in: *Journal of Social History*, 9, 1975, pp. 129–53, and KELLY-GADOL, Joan, 'The Social Relations of the Sexes: Methodical Implications of Women's History', in: *Signs*, 11, 1978, pp. 217–23.

TILLY, Louise and SCOTT, Joan, *Women, Work and Family*, New York: Holt, Rinehart & Winston, 1978, provides good bibliographical tips for further study. On the new status of women due to the changes that occurred in America in the first quarter of the nineteenth century, LERNER, Gerda, 'The Lady and the Mill Girl: Changes in the Status of Women in the Age of Jackson', in: *American Studies*, Vol. 10, no. 1, 1969, pp. 5–15, is concise and clear. The Oxford University Women's Studies Committee has brought out two collections of seminar papers, valuable for the history of housework: ARDENER, Shirley, Editor *Defining Females: The Nature of Women in Society*, London: Croom Helm, 1978; and BURMAN, Sandra, Editor *Fit Work for Women*, London: Croom Helm, 1979. Each contribution is well annotated.

Not only in the home did female work become, in a unique way, distinct from what men do. Also where women were employed for wages, new kinds of work were created and primarily reserved for women. HAUSEN, Karin, 'Technischer Fortschritt und Frauenarbeit im 19.Jh.: zur Sozialgeschichte der Naehmaschine,' in: *Geschichte und Gesellschaft*, Year 4, No. 4, 1978, pp. 148–69, describes how the sewing machine that could have made the household more independent from the market was, in fact, used to increase exploitative wage labor defined as female work. DAVIES, M., 'Woman's place is at the Typewriter: The feminization of the Clerical Labor Force', in: *Radical America*, Vol. 8, no. 4, July–Aug. 1974, pp. 1–28, makes a similar analysis of the use of the typewriter around which an unprecedented army of secretaries was organized. On the reorganization of prostitution around the services of medicine and police, see: CORBIN, Alain, *Les filles de noce: misère sexuelle et prostitution aux XIX° et XX° siècles*, Paris: Aubier Coll. Historique, 1978. On the prehistory of the ideal of the houswife see HOOD, Sarah Jane R., *The Impact of Protestantism on the Renaissance Ideal of Women in Tudor England*, PhD Thesis, Lincoln, 1977. From abstract: "The feminine ideal of wife and mother appears for the first time among Northern humanists in the Renaissance. Studia Humanitis were the key to the successful fulfillment of the domestic role as learned wife to a companion husband, and intelligent guide to education of children. This upper class ideal replaced medieval ideal of virgin or courtly Lady. The protestant ideal of calling made the domestic ideal the vocation of all women in Tudor England. All women were now called to the married state, and could make no finer contribution than to bear children. The home maker replaced the Renaissance companion. The lowliest household tasks a worthy contribution to godly society. But when all were called to matrimony and motherhood, then women were called to nothing else. To choose other, was to deny their holy vocation. Thus the domestic ideal became dogmatized."

One of the principal means by which society imposed recently defined work on women through its agents, the caring professions, is the ideal of 'motherly care'. How mothering became an unpaid, professionally supervised kind of shadow work can be followed through: LOUX, Francoise, *Le jeune enfant et son corps dans la médecine traditionnelle*, Paris: Flammarion, 1978; BARDET, J. P., 'Enfants abandonnés et enfants assistés à Rouen dans la seconde moitié du XVIII° siècle', in: *Hommage à Racel Reinhard*, Paris 1973, pp. 19–48. Flandrin comments: "La seule étude permettant actuellement de mesurer les dangers de l'allaitement mercenaire pour les enfants de famille"; GELIS, J., LAGET, M. and MOREL, M. F., *Entrer dans la vie: naissances et enfances dans la France traditionnelle*, Paris, 1978; OTTMUELLER, Uta, ' "Mutter-pflichten": Die Wandlungen ihrer inhaltlichen Ausformung durch die akademische Medizin', pp. 1–47, MS 1979, with excellent selective bibliography; LALLEMENT, Suzanne and DELAISI DE PARSEVAL, Geneviève, 'Les joies du maternage de 1950 à 1978, ou Les vicissitudes des brochures officielles de puériculture', in: *Les Temps Modernes*, Oct. 1978, pp. 497–550; BADINTE, Elisabeth, *L'amour en plus*, Paris: Flammarion, 1980.

POULOT, Denis, *Le sublime ou le travailleur comme il est en 1870, et ce qu'il peut être*, Introduction by Alain Cottereau, Paris: Francois Maspero, 1980. A small factory owner of Paris, himself a former worker, tries in 1869 to develop a typology of 'workers' and how each type behaves toward his boss and his wife.

OAKLEY, Ann, *Woman's Work: The Housewife, Past and Present*, New York: Vintage Book, 1976, deals in the 7th chapter extensively with these three myths.

Clifford GEERTZ, in a review of D. SYMON, *The Evolution of Human Sexuality*, Oxford University Press, 1980, published in *The New York Review of Books*, 24 Jan. 1980. See also HUBBARD, R. et al. *Women look at Biology*, Boston: Hall, 1979.

To page 109

NAG, Moni, 'An Anthropological Approach to the Study of the Economic Values of Children in Java and Nepal', in: *Current Anthropology*, 19, 2, 1978, pp. 293–306, gives also general bibliography on the economic imputation of value to family members.

BECKER, Gary S., 'A Theory of Marriage', in: *Journal of Political Economy*, 81, 1973, pp. 813–46, and *The Economic Approach to human behavior*, Univ. of Chicago Press, 1976. LEPAGE, H., *Autogestion et capitalisme*, Paris: Masson, 1978.

To page 110

SKOLKA, Jiti V., 'The Substitution of Self-Service activities for Marketed Services', in: *Review of Income and Wealth*, Ser. 22, 4, 1976, p. 297ff., argues as follows: self-service activities are defined as activities carried out outside the market, having as inputs consumer time, industrial products (mainly durables) and often energy. Increasingly these self-service activities are substituted for marketed services. Thus an increasing part of activities in industrialized countries are productive, yet cannot be recorded by conventional economic measures, since they neither appear on the market nor have market value. Unless the value of self-service, substituted for marketed values, is included in the measurement of the nation's welfare, this measurement becomes meaningless. Yet, any recording of self-service activities implies large-scale imputations, a procedure disliked by statisticians.